Imagine

Jesus...

FRANK ANDERSEN, MSC

LIGUORI
PUBLICATIONS

One Liguori Drive
Liguori, MO 63057-9999
(314) 464-2500

Nihil Obstat: Rev. Dr. Mark Coleridge, L.S.S., D.S.S., Diocesan Censor
Imprimatur: Rev. Mons. Gerald A. Cudmore, Vicar General
Date: March 22, 1994

ISBN 0-89243-921-1
Library of Congress Catalog Card Number: 96-75851

Originally published in 1994 as *Jesus: Our Story* by Collins Dove, an imprint of
HarperCollins*Melbourne,* 22–24 Joseph Street, North Blackburn, Victoria 3130,
Australia.

Excerpts from *The New Jerusalem Bible,* copyright © 1985 by Darton, Longman
& Todd, Ltd. and Doubleday & Company, Inc., a division of Bantam Doubleday
Dell Publishing Group, Inc. Reprinted by permission.

Printed in the United States of America
00 99 98 97 96 5 4 3 2 1

Cover design by Chris Sharp

To my mother, who lived so much of this,
long before I found the courage to put words to it.

Contents

Jesus, the Human One

An Autobiographical Note

This book presents some aspect of how one person's understanding of Jesus has changed and deepened over fifty years of life. Experience tells me it is no final word. Nor would it claim to be the only way of seeing Jesus. The mystery of who he is remains greater than any one person's experience or grasp. As well, as I've grown older, my experience of Jesus has moved through at least two major stages of understanding. I hope it will evolve even further.

Nevertheless, if my wider reading and observations are valid, the changes I speak of here represent an experience shared by others as well.

Currently within the Church one can sense a struggle concerning the relationship between Jesus' divinity and his humanity. Perhaps, for Christians, this is the never-ending struggle of faith: that when all is said and done, and no matter how uncomfortable the question, we must all of us ask ourselves, *What actually is the meaning of Incarnation?* It seems that every aspect of Christian faith quite literally depends on how we see this crucial and fundamental issue. We shouldn't be afraid to probe its meaning.

Let me say from the outset and not defensively that the divinity of Jesus forms the deepest and most solid core of my faith in him. It is not in question.

My question concerns *our encounter* with such divinity. It is my conviction that the divine reality at the heart of Jesus is discovered, revealed, and finally known only by facing squarely the fiercest dimensions of his humanness.

In other words, we believe that the human heart of this extraordinary person, Jesus, is actually a window onto God.

Even more, it is our conviction that the human heart of any one of us is like a library of God, and that to explore the deeper levels of any person's experience of life is to run that ultimate risk of coming face-to-face with the God Jesus knew. Thus, Jesus is living proof of how close God is to any one of us. The conviction of Christian faith is that every human person has access to this God whom Jesus experienced. Indeed, it is the basis of Jewish faith that every person carries the image and likeness of this God within his or her heart. This is very good news.

> The glory of God is a person fully alive.
> —Saint Irenaeus

> If you wish to discover God, then go by way of the human one.
> —Saint Augustine

Situating the Question

Like many Catholics, I began my faith life with a childlike commitment to Jesus and to the stories of the gospel. In those days one didn't use the name of Jesus lightly. The preferred terminology was "Our Lord," or, as I remember mission and retreat priests calling him, "Our divine Master." These are lovely terms, and I have no argument with them. But when they alone formed the currency of our relationship with Jesus, then it is no surprise that he became a distant (if sacred) figure. The names we used of him made it difficult for us to imagine him as a friend: he was "Lord," and he was "somehow different."

I spent childhood and a fair amount of adulthood in relating to a Jesus who was unlike us. He did wonderful, unheard-of things called miracles, which "proved he was divine." He possessed powers that I could conceive of only as special, even magical. Nor was the art surrounding us in those days helpful. He was pictured constantly as being different from those around him, whether by halo, by light, by posture or gesture. He was *The One,* and unlike him, we were battlers. In my childish mind, Jesus *knew,* while we had to struggle on in faith as best we could.

There is a truth in this, but it is by no means the entire truth.

For me, problems with the faith began then with questions like these: if Jesus looked and acted so special, if Jesus was so divinely sure of himself, then how was it possible for those who knew him so well to misread him so completely? How would it ever have been possible for his disciples to cut and run when the times were testing? And I confess to having always felt a dangerous sympathy for poor Judas: surely, if Jesus knew everything from the beginning—as I believed—then calling Judas as a disciple was a little unfair, a little like "cornering" him in his destiny.

One of my earliest memories of the nativity saw Jesus lying in the manger with the full consciousness of God. There he realized calmly and lucidly that he would be around for all of thirty years and in that same moment was conscious that his parents knew nothing of what would be. And *that story* of how he confounded the Temple doctors at the age of twelve added gospel verification to my childlike perceptions. He clearly knew more than they did. He was simply "letting it out" bit by bit. The miracles, of course, were seen as clear proof of his extraordinary powers, for only God could do the things he did.

Parents and teachers had nourished me in a faith that was appropriate to a child's mind. They had introduced me well to this greatest of all mysteries, the Incarnation of God. It became life's pleasant task to round off that education so well begun. And happily, this educative journey coincided with the outpourings of biblical scholarship, both Protestant and Catholic.

Learning about the Scriptures during seminary years was like entering an old familiar world through a new doorway. But in some ways the deeper fruits of those years of study only became apparent in the rediscovery of scriptural prayer through the 1970s and 1980s. In study one learned *about* Jesus; but in prayer, *one met him*. It would be difficult now to name all to whom I am indebted for the faith. To thank them adequately is beyond me. Realization began to dawn that this is indeed what being a Church is all about: it is our pleasant task to pass on, generation to generation, the truth of Jesus.

This is not, however, the total story of those years. There was also operating in me a gift of imagination and intuition somewhat like a second level of understanding. Its language was poetry and music. Through the 1970s I began exploring this new capacity, mainly by writing songs about life's experience and, a little later, songs about Jesus. I can still recall the evening when a particular insight dawned.

I had been writing about the experience of aloneness in the priesthood. The third verse of this early song was as follows:

> And have you ever wandered lost along the lonely streets of life,
>   looking for some long-forgotten home?
> No friend to ease the hollow pain that eats away your heart...
>   no footsteps but your own to fill the night?
> Well, it's then *you hear the words of Christ* about foxes and birds;
>   you realise that you're a man apart...
> Although loneliness can tear apart the essence of a man,
>   it cannot touch the embers of your heart.

I remember clearly the moment of awesome realization that with the merest change to the words of line three, the whole song took on a different dimension of meaning:

Well, it's then *your words come back to you* about foxes and birds...

With this one change the whole song, all three verses, became a song not about myself, but about the Jesus I was coming to know.

The words rang true. It was as if, suddenly, we did have something in common, he and I—some bridge of common experience between our otherwise separated lives. We both had known the human experience of aloneness and the implications of a committed life—his fully, mine hesitantly.

It began to dawn on me that when Jesus spoke about foxes and birds' having nowhere to lay their heads, he was speaking from nothing other than his lived experience. His *experience* was the source of that unusual authority at which people marveled; he *knew* the things about which he spoke. He spoke only of the things he *knew*.

Human Experience As a Way to God

Only much later would I begin to notice words actually written into the New Testament that clearly indicated what for me, at that moment, had been a novel discovery: Jesus was actually like us. The letter to the Hebrews (2:17–18) emphatically states how essential it was that Jesus was "completely like" us, otherwise he could never have become that "compassionate and trustworthy high priest" so necessary in forging our correct "relationship to God." This important letter argues that it was "the suffering he himself passed through while being put to the test" that rendered him capable of understanding the human struggle and suffering of us all.

In a sense, Catholics are only now rediscovering the richness of the Scriptures. It has been labeled one of the enduring achievements of Vatican Council II that the Scriptures are again in our hands. The Church has done this mainly through the restored readings of the liturgy. Sadly, the Scriptures' being so available does not automatically mean that they are fully a part of our inner lives and belief. It remains a task for us to develop that "warm and living love of scripture" that the Church holds to be so important if we are to measure up to these times. This reevangelization of the Church itself is seen as a central task today.

Let me mention a second passage from Hebrews: "For the high priest we have is not incapable of feeling our weaknesses with us, but has been put to the test in exactly the same way as ourselves, apart from sin" (4:15).

In earlier years, the last phrase of this passage dominated our understanding. Sin was so central to Catholic consciousness that if it was something that Jesus did *not* have (and we did), then he was clearly unlike us in our struggles, our limits, and our failings. The way we understood sin limited our capacity to understand Jesus.

However, when we realize the scriptural understanding of the term *sin,* the above passage takes on powerful meaning. For the term used in Scripture for *sin* is a word that literally means "to miss the mark" or "to be wide of target." It has its origins in archery: an arrow either hits or misses the target. Jesus never "missed the target"; he never "missed the point" of his life. He was tempted just as you and I are tempted—even more severely. But through it all, when it came down to the wire, he kept saying, "Yes!" to his God, to others in his life, and to the love he had publicly committed himself to live. He never sinned. He never said, "Enough!" He never said, "I cannot and will not continue!"

The religious congregation to which I belong has a special interest in studying the heart of this man, Jesus. We are fascinated (captured, if you will) by what drove him.

In a past era this was called *Devotion to the Sacred Heart.* Such a title is not easily understood today. It was a language for understanding Jesus and his quality of heart that became popular in Europe during recent centuries. It was a way of speaking about

God's love that suited those times and, in our congregation's case, it was very French. Over recent years, such language has come to carry less and less weight with Australians like myself.

During the 1960s and 1970s, we began trying to better express the insight of this "devotion." What was it really about? We tried to express who Jesus was by using a language that would make sense to people of today.

The basic conviction is that God could be found at the deepest core of Jesus. And he was like us.

So let us begin to understand what drove his life and so catch a sense of the ideals that filled him. Let us begin to sense the dreams that inspired him and appreciate the defeats that humanized him. Were we to do this, then we would be on the way to understanding not only Jesus, but also God. This has become my conviction.

A prayerful reading of the gospel stories is crucial to gaining that insight, for these stories were written by those who knew him well. The gospels portray a person whom the writers never wanted to forget. This is how they remembered him. Yet there remains one caution to keep in mind as we begin a study of the gospel stories, a caution that humbles and alerts us: what we "see" in a gospel story depends in large measure on what has been our experience of life.

Experience tells us that when we read gospel stories, we notice in them only what we are capable of noticing. As *our* human experience deepens, so are we able to notice increasingly the more subtle characteristics of this profoundly human person. In other words, *our* lives and human experience are like keys that release the perception of what is written into the gospels.

Jesus had a human heart, and so have we. To understand and explore *our* human heart's experience of life is in some way to understand and explore his. Our hearts give us access to the heart of God. This also is good news.

This book does not attempt an academic treatment of the gospel passages we use. Such scholarship can be found in more appropriate places. This is simply a sharing of one person's story and growing insight. It is by no means the whole story. I hope it will help your own prayerful reading of similar gospel passages. Such quiet and prayerful reading is one important way of coming to know the person of Jesus.

In the Bulletin for the April 1992 Australian Catholic Bishops' Conference, there is mention of a new committee that they have formed, called the Committee for Evangelization and Missions. The Bulletin quotes Father Gino Henriques, C.SS.R., Director of *Evangelization 2000* for the Asian Region and a visitor to the 1992 Conference:

> Perhaps the biggest task may very well be that of inspiring *active Catholics* to fall in love with Jesus, to be converted to him, to make him central to their lives, to imitate him and to share their experience of him with others.

I have added the emphasis. This is a powerful challenge, and it is in the spirit of that challenge that this sharing of gospel experience is offered.

What Kind of Book Is This?

THIS BOOK IS INTENDED to be simple and uncomplicated. It makes no claim to be an academic study of either Jesus or the Scriptures. It is rather the fruit of one person's years of praying and pondering gospel stories.

These pages represent a meeting point between the person who emerges from behind the gospel stories and my own experience of an all-too-human life. This book concerns the Jesus I have met in gospel-prayer and whom, over fifty years of faith, I have come to know as a companion in life.

The Jesus who emerges in these pages is the fruit of my imagination—that extraordinary, divine capacity we all possess but so frequently undervalue. Only in our imagination do we "build a coherent picture" out of the many different influences on our lives: our reading and study, our reflection and prayer, our hard-won experience, and those people who affect us deeply. It's in our imagination that we "put it all together" and make sense of things—we imagine what God is like, and we imagine what life is about.

In this profoundly Christian sense I have played imaginatively with the gospel stories through my life. This is a form of prayer that has a lengthy Christian tradition. Saint Teresa of Avila would sit Jesus down—in her imagination—before her in an empty chair and simply speak and listen to him, using her heart's eye. Saint

Ignatius of Loyola built his retreat program around such imaginative encounters with Jesus.

In such prayer one goes beyond the mere text of the Scriptures into the world of imagination where one meets the Jesus portrayed there. These prayer-based images give focus and energy to one's life— yet they also change as we mature. Childhood images rarely sustain adult faith. Adult experience permits deeper insight into who Jesus was, and deeper appreciations of the undercurrents of his life.

Every believer carries imaginary pictures of Jesus: how we imagine him determines how we relate to him. Did he walk this earth as a God or as a human person? Was he really *like* us? Or was he different? How does *his* life connect with ours? These are the serious questions facing us today.

The way Jesus lived is a pattern for all of us. He embodies for us what it means to be filled by God. In his life we see expressed the deepest human potential. In other words, he *did* what all of us would love to do if only we possessed his courage and faith. In him we see the reason for existence.

In the truest sense of the word, this makes Jesus our myth. That is, he alone is the meaning of our lives. If we want to know who we are and what life is about, then look only at Jesus and at how he lived. He alone is the key. He is the Way, he is the Truth, he is the Life. He alone is the foundation and myth of our lives.

Sadly, we have lost this lovely meaning to the word *myth*. But for the Greeks, who coined the term, myths were truths (sometimes told in stories) that gave meaning and value to life. To call Jesus our myth is to place him squarely at the heart and center of human life. In other words, Jesus is our story.

Imaginative Gospel Prayer

THE WAY OF PRAYING with the gospels I describe here provides a model through which we may encounter Jesus imaginatively. It enables us to speak with him, to listen to him, and to situate *his* story alongside *our* story as we search for meaning in our lives.

- Read several times the small passage of the gospel that you wish to pray. Let it come inside you so that you no longer need the book. Read it slowly and deliberately into your memory, enjoying doing so. Some phrases stay in your mind more easily than others.

Put the gospel book aside once this prayerful reading is done.

- Calmly imagine that you yourself are in the scene you are memorizing. Sometimes it helps to picture in your mind's eye some of the surroundings:

    —what sort of day is it?
    —what time of day is it?
    —what can you see around you?
    —what sounds can you hear?

Many find it helpful to close their eyes when doing this.

It seems important to sit quietly and still.

Some find it helpful to remember a scene from their own life that is *like* the scene of the gospel: perhaps a room in your own home, or a favorite park; or some loved memory of a place of your childhood, or of a special moment by the sea, or of an evening.

Be creative at this stage of the prayer.

It is a little like dreaming a scene in your mind's eye and enjoying it as you do.

When ready, place yourself in that scene alongside Jesus.

Perhaps there are others around as well, but make sure that he knows *you* are there and that he knows your name well.

Whenever he speaks with you, hear him using your name.

- As you imagine the gospel scene, the prayer begins.

In your imagination, quietly let happen what the gospel story is about.

Watch what is occurring.

Listen to what is said and to *how* it is said. Play some words over and over in your mind until you hear them spoken just as you imagine they *were* spoken at the time.

Notice with great care anything that begins to move you or affect you in any way. Pay very careful attention to this if it happens.

Quietly and calmly replay such moments over and over in your imagination.

Let them change if necessary.

Let such moments work their way into your heart.

This is called "tasting the text."

- Sometimes nothing will happen. Sometimes one's prayer is dry. Be calm and patient if this occurs. Prayer is not what *we* do, but something that *God* does in us.

  We pray like farmers preparing the soil: we do our bit and then wait, patiently wait for the rains to come.

  Only God brings rain.

  But we wait in confidence too, for God wants to communicate with us and will do so when we are most open to noticing God's presence.

  Often we are most open when we are least prepared.

  Prayer is not something we can turn on whenever we choose, but we wait quietly, pondering and tasting the gospel passage we have chosen and allowing it to filter through our imagination.

- Remember, when something starts to affect you, let your mind quietly focus on that word, phrase, or image. Let everything else go.

- When you feel you have had enough, open your eyes and return gently to your normal surroundings.

  Before you move away, be sure to thank God in some short, genuine way for the privilege of knowing Jesus.

Stand Up and Be Counted

It was at this time that Jesus came from Nazareth in Galilee and was *baptised* in the Jordan by John. And at once, as he was coming up out of the water, he saw the heavens torn apart and *the Spirit, like a dove, descending on him.* And a voice came from heaven, "You are my Son, the Beloved; my favour rests on you."...And at once *the Spirit drove him into the desert* and he remained there for *forty* days, and was put to the test by Satan.

Mark 1:9–12 (emphasis added)

Jesus, *with the power of the Spirit in him,* returned to Galilee; and his reputation spread throughout the countryside. He taught in their synagogues and everyone glorified him.

Luke 4:14–15 (emphasis added)

THE BAPTISM OF JESUS is fascinating. Not so much *how* it happened, but *that* it happened at all, or even that it happened *when* it did.

Jesus had lived in his society for thirty years. He must have been aware of what was going on around him. His society was deeply divided, just as ours is increasingly becoming.

The family of Jesus, although poor, was "acceptable." They attended synagogue. Each year they journeyed to the Temple in Jerusalem to offer sacrifice and to pay their respects. Because they were at the poorer end of society, their Temple offering consisted simply of two turtledoves. They hadn't the means to purchase and offer the bulls, heifers, calves, or sheep that wealthier people could afford.

As well, Jesus seemed to be at home in attending the local synagogue of the smaller townships. His family, in short, was a "good and respectable" family; they might have been poor, but they lived on the right side of the railway line, so to speak.

Sadly, his type of family represented only one part of the story of those times. The gospels show us with distressing clarity a whole wash of humanity considered to be little more than social garbage.

The Sick

Illness, especially of a disfiguring nature, was seen by many as a punishment from God. We even find Jesus' own disciples asking, "'Rabbi, who sinned, this man or his parents, that he should have been born blind?'" (John 9:2).

Many presumed that the crippled, the blind, the mute, and the leprous were somehow, in some unknown way, suffering now for sins and moral failure in their lives. It was as if the illness made evident to all their unworthiness before God.

And so they were shunned. Their sufferings were doubled by this harsh presumption that they somehow deserved what they were going through. They were treated as social outcasts.

The Insane

The general term *possessed by devils* illustrates clearly the harshness of society's judgment on such people. The violently insane "had to stay outside in places where nobody lived," in the cemeteries and among the tombs or quarries on the edge of town. To their illness was added this social rejection.

Sinners

Sinners was a general term used to describe all those who, for whatever reason, were unable to live according to the codes of the "religious" people of the day—too poor to offer sacrifice (the widow's small coin) or too unkempt to dare enter a synagogue.

Perhaps they were too well known for their sinful lives: prostitutes, beggars, and those who stole for a living. The gospels refer many times to such "well-known sinners."

Tax Collectors

Levi was one of the tax collectors. They were Jews who had the franchise to collect taxes for Rome from their own Jewish people. The Romans were experienced enough to know that the one who actually takes your money is the one hated, so they let Jews do this for them. Tax collectors lived off a percentage of the takings. Some, like Zacchaeus, were generous in such estimations! Other Jews treated them as traitors and low-life collaborators: working-dogs of a Rome they despised.

Outcasts

The general term *outcasts* covers all of the above and simply describes their actual experience of being forbidden to enter God's Temple or synagogue. This tide of humanity was the "underside" of Jewish society.

Every society spawns its equivalent, and ours is no exception. These were the disinherited, the prisoners, the poor. Often, especially in Mark's Gospel, they are collectively called "the crowd."

Unless we have some appreciation of the social setting of Jesus' life, we will never understand who he was. Nor will we appreciate the gospel meaning of the word *salvation*.

The gospels tell us that because of the Roman occupation of Palestine, there were an immense number of landless peasants. Taxes were crippling. Opposition to the Roman regime was severely repressed. During the time of the childhood of Jesus, hundreds who had revolted in Galilee had been crucified along the roadway between Nazareth and Capernaum. Violence simmered in times when the rich prospered and masses of people were dispossessed.

Jesus had lived for thirty years in such a world. He could see for himself what was going on. This was no longer the nation that had pledged itself at Sinai to be God's holy people. There they had promised to enshrine in the Law the rights and dignity of all, even the poorest of the poor. The magnificent religious vision of the covenant had been compromised. The world in which Jesus matured was no longer the world of God's covenanted people.

He would have known at firsthand the extent of the injustice, and seen for himself the realities of poverty. He would have known intimately the endless cycle of injustice and disesteem that missed entirely the point of God's loving covenant. He would have sensed clearly the anger, the resentment, and the profound disillusionment in many hearts. He would have seen his beloved Israel caught in the ravages of sin.

Jesus grew up among the outsiders, those marginal people who lived their lives of quiet desperation. His heart told him the wrongness of it all. He learned to recognize the human face of sin and how his beloved nation had "missed the point" on God's love.

Perhaps the wonder of it all is that it took Jesus so many years to make up his mind to do something about it. In the overall pattern of his life, so much of his time was spent in Nazareth, silent and hidden and uncommitted. When we realize this, surely there is hope for us all.

Baptism was to be his public commitment. No longer would he stay out of the public arena of confrontation and dangerous struggle. He would become a protagonist; he would signify that publicly. He, who had grown up as part of the establishment, would cross that dangerous social boundary and freely keep company with "the nobody people." Believing in their profound sacredness, he would eat and mix with them.

His life would thus illustrate the shape of God's desired kingdom. By enjoying their company, he would convince them of their inner value. Words were cheap; it was action that was needed. He refused to treat them as outsiders. There could be no intolerance or exclusion in the kingdom of the God he knew. He would show this by his lifestyle.

Once baptized, all who knew him could call him to account for the commitment baptism represented. It was an irreversible, public gesture. From this moment, he was "in."

Baptism is a Greek word. It has meanings that are precise and rich. Primarily, it means "to be overwhelmed"—to be totally submerged in the truth of something, to be swept off one's feet by something or by someone. In this sense, Jesus was "blown away" by the Baptist's insight and courage. He could no longer resist the pressure of John's teaching and life. He would symbolize this by being baptized by John.

For Jesus, as indeed for anyone, baptism was a moment of conversion, of turning even more deliberately to his God.

It is important to notice that only after he had found the courage to make this public declaration did he know in his bones the affirmation of God's special choice and love. God is never outdone in generosity. When Jesus took that dangerous choice of committing himself to "true kingdom," he knew in a deeper way the commitment God made in return.

His decisiveness released the Spirit within himself. It was as if the Spirit, lying somehow dormant within him over these years, was stirred to emerge. Jesus was learning to surrender his life to the Spirit seeded deep within. He was learning to be attentive at all levels of his being.

Just as the apostles were to become decisive, courageous, and energetic builders of Church at Pentecost, so likewise did the Spirit build Jesus into apostolic strength and vigor. The Spirit lying deep in this potent human being was released, and how it flowed! Jesus became an extension of Spirit. That "image of God" in which all human persons are made was, in Jesus, allowed to emerge, given voice to speak, and ultimately allowed to fashion him. He began thereby to embody and to live the human person's fullest potential. The image of God was taking flesh.

Unlike most of us, Jesus chose to be undefended against this eruption of his deepest, true Spirit. In Jesus we see what happens when we allow the Spirit its way.

His was an extraordinary conversion. The handing over of his life to Spirit was total. We glimpse here the degree of surrender that alone frees the inner God and that makes the space needed for God to take flesh. It is a "death" to hand over one's life like this into the power of God. Yet it was the only way possible for Jesus to discover his deepest, hidden self. His life portrayed the beautiful contradiction that human surrender alone can bring true freedom. In his life we see embodied the hope we all possess.

Jesus was divine because he was so totally human. He learned to live at that profound depth of personhood where access to the divine is possible. He revealed the potential of us all. It is a dangerous, if lovely, potential.

This Spirit drove him into the wilderness. Not just momentarily, but for forty days. The number *forty* crops up on several important occasions in the Bible. It rained in the Noah story for forty days and nights. The Israelites wandered through the desert for forty years. Elijah walked for forty days and forty nights until he reached Horeb, the mountain of God. Lent is forty days in length. The number is a Hebrew code for the whole of one's life.

And so it was for Jesus. The decision he made at his baptism rendered him publicly committed, and this was the beginning of "the wilderness" of his life, the commencement of his years of being "driven by the Spirit."

This Spirit never let him rest. It filled, cajoled, confirmed, and tantalized him always. He would now know the constant temptations to self-glorification, ego, and power. In all of this struggle he never sinned: he never said, "No" or "Enough!" to the deepening demands of love and truth. In this precise sense he never "missed the point" of his life's commitment.

Yet like Jacob of old, Jesus found himself wrestling with God's demands and struggling with God's vision of how things could be. He chose to become implicated in God's plans for justice and truthful speaking. As the letter to the Hebrews would say it, "...he learnt obedience, Son though he was, through his sufferings; when he had been perfected, he became for all who obey him the source of eternal salvation..." (Hebrews 5:8–9).

If this is truly the story of how one human person could be possessed by God's Spirit, then there is hope in the story of Jesus' life for all of us. It no longer matters who we are. It no longer matters how we have spent the previous years of our lives. Jesus embodied human potential. This is one lovely meaning of the teaching that "in him we are saved."

> He is the image of the unseen God,
> the first-born of all creation....
> Colossians 1:15

It should not, therefore, surprise us that in Mark's Gospel Jesus is constantly called "the Son of man." Some commentators prefer to translate this title as "the Human One." It is a way of speaking about Jesus that I find particularly expressive.

The implications for us are enormous. Not that we will ever embody Spirit in the complete way Jesus did, but we are flesh of his flesh and bone of his bone. He became like us. This is the ground of all hope. Jesus can look us right in the eye and tell us that he knows what it's really like. *We* are caught up in *his* deepest reality. He needed to face the issues of his time; he needed to make a public commitment (baptism). So it is for us as well: there is no way but baptism if we wish to mature into God. In this precise sense, Jesus is the Way for us all.

For Prayer

Imagine you are sitting beside Jesus on a hillside. Just down in front of you, John is baptizing people in the River Jordan. You and Jesus have both been watching this for some time, silently. You have been listening to John for days and weeks now as he challenges people to change their hearts and minds, urging people to open their eyes to "see" what is occurring around them. As you listen, you become aware of something happening in Jesus. Something decisive is occurring. He stands and deliberately moves down toward John in the river.

Sense the determination and decision within him and the focus of his mind as he asks for baptism.

For Discussion

- *Baptism* means "to be overwhelmed," or to be totally submerged. A second meaning comes from the dye makers of ancient Greece: to dip a cloth *repeatedly* into the boiling dye until it takes on the right coloring.

  Given these meanings, how do we "overwhelm" people with the story of Jesus today? How many ways are there for us to "tell the story" in today's world?

  The pope and bishops have called the nineties the "Decade of Evangelization." Whom do they have in mind to be evangelized? And what, in practice, do you believe their challenge might mean for us?

- Many years ago, Bishop Flores of San Antonio, Texas, was reported as saying that, in his experience, Catholics in this country have been "sacramentalized, but never evangelized." In other words, we have been taught well how to attend the sacraments, but we have never really been exposed to the gospel of Jesus.

  What is your comment in terms of your own experience of being Catholic?

2
Where You Stand Is What You See

That evening, *after sunset,* they brought to him all who were sick and those who were possessed by devils. *The whole town* came crowding round the door, and he cured many who were sick with diseases of one kind or another; he also drove out many devils, but he would not allow them to speak, because they knew who he was.

In the morning, *long before dawn,* he got up and left the house and *went off to a lonely place* and *prayed* there. Simon and his companions set out in search of him, and when they found him they said, "Everybody is looking for you." He answered, "Let us go elsewhere, to the neighbouring country towns, so that I can proclaim the message there too, because that is why I came." And he went all through Galilee, preaching in their synagogues and driving out devils.

Mark 1:32–39 (emphasis added)

MARK'S GOSPEL IS IN many ways a gospel for the nineties. It was the first of the gospels to be written. It can also be called the most basic of the gospels. It is a gospel that talks about Jesus as "the Human One." The Hebrew term for this, *Son of man,* occurs many times in the text.

This is not to suggest that for Mark, Jesus was not divine. Quite the contrary. He began the first sentence of his gospel by calling Jesus "the Son of God." He also used the same term once more in his gospel, as Jesus died. But apart from these two references—and key references they are—Mark seems to have concentrated on the humanness of this man Jesus. In his gospel Mark presented to us a

Jesus with whom we can easily identify, a real person we can follow.

The passage above is taken from Mark's first chapter, where he gave us a delightful description of a typical day in Jesus' life. For Mark, something such as this must have happened early in Jesus' public commitment. This first chapter describes the sort of Jesus who captured Mark's heart.

It is a lovely scene, beginning after sunset as darkness falls. It might sound romantic, but we need to know why Mark even bothered to mention such things as darkness and sunset. We need to know that the society of Jesus' day was different from ours. Especially was it different for the sick, the mad, and the disfigured, who were seen as being punished by God.

Worse, if the disease was contagious, then anyone so afflicted was banished from normal family life, from their jobs, and from their usual social settings. Given the primitive medicine of the times, all human contact had to be avoided. During hours of daylight, such people were banished from the townships. As the sun set and darkness fell, the townspeople retired to their homes, and the streets belonged to the sick. They were the people of the night. It was time to scavenge for food or to collect the offerings of clothing and food and medicine that their families and friends would leave for them on their doorsteps.

The desperately ill of these times were fiercely isolated. They were true outcasts in this society. The rejection and suffering of the disfigured and the insane must have broken the hearts of so many of the sick themselves, and also the hearts of their family and friends.

Of course, Jesus had watched this through all the years of his life in Nazareth. But now he had committed himself publicly to work at making God's kingdom visible and real. He could not but respond to the desperation of such isolated and alienated people. For in the mind of Jesus the realization was dawning that in God's true kingdom there are no outcasts.

No matter what it would cost him in the eyes of others, he could no longer ignore or avoid doing something practical about this distressing reality that was hidden by day but rampant by night. He could no longer avoid noticing society's "invisible people."

Jesus was in town. The whole town came crowding around his door. It was an extraordinary scene: they seemed suddenly to realize that no one but Jesus could possibly heal this weeping social sore. This was their one chance, their one and only hope of something being different. They had heard about him. He got things done. He was afraid of no one. He treated the disfigured, the sick, and the mad with a sacredness and dignity that they experienced nowhere else. He gave them hope.

Jesus went out into the night and moved among them. We know not the details of what he did or of how he spoke. But the experience of that night had a profound effect on Jesus. As Mark told it, Jesus was permanently changed after this night. This was an encounter with suffering, with desperation, and with basic human need. His eyes were opened.

Unable to sleep, restless and harried by what he had encountered, Jesus rose from his bed and walked alone into the surrounding hills. He needed to be with his God. He needed to come to terms with something profound. He was driven into prayer. He had no choice but to try to make some sense out of that night's experience.

He had experienced two things: first, the horror and desperation of so many broken people, as if on that night he had glimpsed for the first time in his life the full extent of human need and suffering. He could avoid the reality no longer. Worse, this was only one town. Jesus was overwhelmed by the enormity of the injustice.

But second, and perhaps just as disturbing for him, was the experience of being able to touch that need in some way. He had been able to make a difference. He had within himself the capability to soothe, to reassure, to look these people in the eye and to restore to them their truest, deepest dignity as children of his God. In his compassion he possessed a power. It was a power urgently needed.

These twin realizations drove Jesus to prayer. Confronted by the night's experience, he could not sleep but had to make some sense of what was happening to him. He needed to find his peace in front of that night's revelation.

We know nothing of how Jesus prayed. The fact that he *had* to pray is awesome in itself. We do know that he was in prayer for a long time: from "long before dawn" until Peter woke and went searching for him. It seems that his disciples were already accustomed to the long hours that Jesus spent in prayer. They had a fair idea of where he might be—in the hills.

While we know little of the manner of his praying, we do know the focus of those hours alone: Jesus was coming to see his life more clearly.

Peter encouraged him to return to the village of the previous night, to meet again in daylight those whom he had encountered in the darkness: "'Everybody is looking for you.'"

But in his prayer, Jesus appears to have realized that what he saw that night was the merest glimpse of his nation's massive neediness. What he had suddenly seen was going on in every village and township. Perhaps even worse. To be true to his heart, he must get going. There was now an urgency in him to move out and dedicate himself to this great need.

He could no longer avoid its existence. Nor could he any longer dodge his God-given capacity to touch it and in some ways "heal" it. He was confronted, he was called, both by the need and by his sense of compassion.

His response was courageous and energetic: "'Let us go elsewhere, to the neighbouring country towns, so that I can proclaim the message there too, because that is why I came.'"

Jesus, in this portrait, was someone very like ourselves. Life was his teacher. He had to listen very carefully to what was happening to him. He obviously understood that God "spoke" to him through the things he noticed and experienced. And like us, he clearly had to work his way into the next step of his life. It was in this process, in this fidelity, that he found his fullest freedom and his God.

For Prayer

Imagine you are with Jesus that morning "long before dawn" as he sits quietly in prayer. Sense the memories he holds from the previous night. How are these memories affecting him? Sense within yourself something of how he is being moved. Notice what is happening to your sense of who he is.

Or...

You are sitting with him a few days later, just the two of you, perhaps having something to drink together. You know that the night described above was a turning point in his life. You respectfully ask him, "What happened to you that night, Jesus? What did it all mean for you?"

And you listen as he responds.

For Discussion

- As we struggle to understand how Jesus was human and divine, Catholics have at times felt that Jesus would have known God "from the inside," as it were. Many would suggest that he knew all the time that he was God. Yet strangely, the gospel here described him as *having to pray* if he was to understand the next step in his life.

  How does this affect your understanding of Jesus?

  What is changing for you? Have you always seen him like this?

- Why do *you* pray? Is it for reasons similar to those of Jesus as he prays in this moment of his life? What difference does this realization make to your relationship with Jesus?
- This may not be easy for us to do, but let us ask ourselves who might be the "invisible ones" today? Who might be these "children of the night" in our time?

3

Hang the Cost

A man suffering from a virulent skin-disease came to him and pleaded on his knees saying, "If you are willing, you can *cleanse me.*" *Feeling sorry for him,* Jesus stretched out his hand, *touched him* and said to him, "I am willing. Be cleansed." And at once the skin-disease left him and he was cleansed. And at once Jesus sternly *sent him away* and said to him, "Mind you tell no one anything, but go and show yourself to the priest, and make the offering for your cleansing prescribed by Moses as evidence to them." The man went away, but then started freely proclaiming and telling the story everywhere, so that Jesus could *no longer go openly into any town,* but *stayed outside in deserted places.* Even so, people from all around kept coming to him.

Mark 1:40–45 (emphasis added)

THIS FOLLOWS ON IMMEDIATELY from the previous passage in which we saw Jesus committing himself to "go elsewhere" and to get on with the job of doing something practical about the way he understood God's kingdom. Confronted by the need and now committed to the task, he set about it.

Immediately, the implications of his commitment came home to him. This leper was revealing the full dimensions of what it would cost him.

Lepers appear many times in the gospels. This was the one disease that stripped a person of all self-esteem. In those times, leprosy was considered highly contagious. It was terrible to behold;

even worse to fall prey to it. Leprosy was feared and loathed in a way that we, who don't encounter it, find difficult to imagine. It rendered a person increasingly repulsive and usually ended, after years of suffering, alienation, and neglect, in a lonely death.

The term *leprosy* covered many skin disfigurements, and so feared was the disease that strict laws segregated the leper from all manner of social contact. The leper was truly the outcast of society, banished from family and friends, from synagogue and township— the only companionship that of other lepers. This sudden social and emotional loss was one of the most shattering aspects of this disease. If indeed there occurred some remission, some cure, even then the leper could not return to normal social life without receiving a "declaration of cleanliness" from the local priest, who, in those days, was something like our magistrate today. Even when all the sores had long gone and all the scars had long been cured, a leper was still not considered "healed" until this public, official declaration had been given by the priest.

Men were the only wage earners of the day. If it was the man of the house who became leprous, then the family as well could suffer by falling into abject poverty. Lepers were the unwanted ones without rights, without dignity, without hope.

To be cured of leprosy involved much more than mere physical healing. This is important if we are to understand the story before us, because in this story, physical healing was not the basic issue. Just as leprosy took away one's personal standing and social dignity, so to be "cured" meant to have one's whole life restored to possibility again. Here, the leper asked to be cleansed. The Greek word used for cleansing is *katharizein*. It can equally mean "to declare that a person is clean."

The leper—this leper—was desperate. He banked everything on Jesus. That he approached Jesus was very unusual. Only a priest could provide him with a proper "declaration of cleanliness," and Jesus was certainly not a priest. Some commentators suggest that what had happened was that the leper's sores had long since healed and that he had presented himself to the local priest for his "clean bill of health," but that the priest had refused to declare him clean. They suggest that this was what made Jesus so angry: the hardheartedness of those who sat in judgment on these outcasts of society.

It would make sense if this was the case. Why else would the leper have bothered coming to Jesus (who was not a priest) and in utter desperation challenged him with these startling words: "If you are willing, you can declare me clean!" Approaching Jesus represented his final, desperate commitment.

Jesus was deeply affected by the leper's predicament. Some commentators would even suggest that the words should be translated as "stirred to anger." It would make sense.

Jesus was confronted by a realistic but heartless social custom that alienated and isolated these hopeless people precisely when their self-esteem was so battered. He reacted with utter compassion. Almost recklessly, he "touched" the leper with his own hands.

Physical touch—human contact—was the one thing missing in the leper's life. By "touching" him, Jesus treated him as clean. This very gesture "declared him clean." If someone would treat him like this, then indeed he was "declared clean." He was fit for life once more.

By touching him, Jesus indicated that he was not afraid of the possible contagion. He treated the leper as normal. He gave him his proper dignity, treated him as a person once more. In doing so he "touched" more than the leper's *skin*—he touched his longings, his hopes, his human need for self-esteem and worth.

The *real* miracle here was that Jesus treated him with the personal dignity that no one else was game to display. Jesus stood up for him against the system. He put his own life on the line for the leper's sake.

Touching was a dangerous gesture, and Jesus was aware of how serious were the consequences. Social and legal conventions were

clear: even accidental contact with lepers required months of enforced isolation and quarantine. Jesus knew the risk—and still he
touched. Knowing the conventions, he confronted them head-on,
asking the man not to speak of *how* the cure had been done, but
letting it stay as something between themselves; otherwise, the judgment of people would be swift and severe. Should others become
aware of what Jesus had done, the cost would be high.

We can sympathize with the man who spoke about it everywhere, despite Jesus' plea for confidentiality. And once the word
was out that Jesus had "touched" him, thereby going over the
priest's head, the full penalty was enforced. Jesus was himself isolated, marginalized, shunned. This was the price of his compassion: "...Jesus could no longer go openly into any town, but stayed
outside in deserted places."

Jesus had come to see with clarity the ways of his society. He
saw that much of what was occurring was unjust. Brought up in
the Scriptures, he could see that what was happening was no longer
the kingdom of God. The covenant vision of becoming a nation
who would live God's justice had been lost, and he would challenge that loss with everything he had.

By his lifestyle he would demonstrate the inclusiveness of God's
dream for the world. In the mind of Jesus, God's table would be a
table at which all were welcome. It was God's kingdom when all
could find their deepest dignity and be treated with their rightful
sacredness. He simply would not tolerate a social system that
marginalized and diminished persons. Any society that excluded
the unfortunate had nothing in common with the Father he had
come to know.

Jesus chose to act according to his heart and to challenge head-
on the sinful, depersonalizing ways of his day. In doing this, he
became increasingly prepared to pay the price.

For Prayer

Imagine you are sitting and talking quietly with Jesus some evening after this occurred. He can no longer go openly into any of the local townships. Let the realization of this come home to you as you sit near him. Ask him what goes through his mind these days when he recalls the incident of the leper. Is he regretful? What has been the impact of this whole event on his mind and heart? How has it affected him?

This is a contemplative prayer. The point of it is to listen to how *he* responds to your question. Imagine Jesus confiding quietly in you. Listen to *him* speaking.

For Discussion

- Salvation was something that people experienced when they met Jesus. In this personal interaction, something occurred that the Church later came to call "salvation."

  What was the "salvation" experienced by the leper in this story? Does this affect in any way your own understanding of salvation?

- What is the point of this story for us? Who might be some of the "lepers" of our world and society?

4
Dangerous Language

When he returned to Capernaum, some time later word went round that he was in the house; and so many people collected that there was no room left, even in front of the door. He was preaching the word to them when some people came *bringing him a paralytic* carried by four men, but as they could not get the man to him through the crowd, they stripped the roof over the place where Jesus was; and when they had made an opening, they lowered the stretcher on which the paralytic lay. *Seeing their faith,* Jesus said to the paralytic, "My child, *your sins are forgiven.*" Now some scribes were sitting there, and they thought to themselves, "How can this man talk like that? He is being blasphemous. *Who but God can forgive sins?*" And at once, Jesus, *inwardly aware that this is what they were thinking,* said to them, "Why do you have these thoughts in your hearts? Which of these is easier to say to the paralytic, 'Your sins are forgiven' or to say, 'Get up, pick up your stretcher and walk'? But to prove to you that the *Son of man* has authority to forgive sins on earth"—he said to the paralytic—"I order you: get up, pick up your stretcher, and go off home." And the man got up, and at once picked up his stretcher and walked out in front of everyone, so that they were all astonished and praised God saying, "We have never seen anything like this."

Mark 2:1–12 (emphasis added)

THIS IS THE FIRST TIME in Mark's Gospel that Jesus dared to use dangerous words. This human person, this simple and unlettered man, dared to utter words that only God was supposed to utter. Jesus made a public issue about forgiving sin.

To appreciate the impact of this moment, we must know something of the cultural background of the day.

You will remember that at the beginning of the ninth chapter of John's Gospel, Jesus and his disciples were entering the Temple in Jerusalem when they found at the doorway a blind man. His disciples immediately asked of Jesus, "Who sinned? This man or his parents, for him to have been born blind?" (author's paraphrase).

Because the man was blind, the common presumption was that his blindness was some sort of punishment for infidelity, perhaps even his own. For the disciples, the issue was clear: either this man himself had sinned, or it may have been his parents. Either way, blindness was a punishment from God.

Perhaps it surprises us that in those times an ordinary illness or handicap could be seen as some sort of punishment from God. Moral guilt was presumed to lie behind physical illness.

Thanking God for winning the lottery, or cursing God for some misfortune, are children of the same mental attitude. One wonders how alive such attitudes still are today. Jesus simply declared that God's mystery was beyond all such thinking. He would not tolerate such attitudes to the God he loved. Such a God was one whom he could not recognize.

In John's ninth chapter, Jesus charged his disciples not to think like that. Illness and misfortune had nothing to do with the nature of God. The Father Jesus knew was not one to punish. The Father he knew loved only life.

Yet this imputation of immorality was rife in Jesus' time. The paralyzed man of this story was fortunate in having friends who stood by him and who were courageous enough to bring him to Jesus in public. No wonder he admired their *faith*. They were committed to their paralyzed friend.

The mind-set of those who judged the unfortunate angered Jesus. The common presumption of immorality stripped the afflicted of their inner dignity, already made brittle by illness. He would have none of such viciousness. Emboldened by the courage he had seen, Jesus himself decided to live dangerously in the service of the truth in which he believed. He took to himself the authority reserved to God alone—he spoke out for justice, and he spoke in God's name: "Your sins are dismissed, gone, thrown aside, and of no account! There is no sin here" (author's paraphrase).

The challenge was unbelievable. That a human person would dare to take upon himself the prerogative of God was far more amazing than the eventual physical cure.

In daring to speak like this, Jesus confronted conventions both social and religious. Driven by his vision of God's justice, he refused to tolerate the presumption that punishment for some past action lay at the cause of a person's paralysis. No matter what it cost him, he would speak his mind and declare his conviction. It was as if, as the paralyzed man slowly arrived via the skylight, Jesus wanted to clear the ground of any misconceptions that might possibly have lurked in the room. He simply declared, as if to set the record straight from the outset, "There is no question of sin here" (author's words).

It is often easy for us to momentarily forget that Jesus was a Jew. He thought like any Jewish person of his day. And the foundation of all Jewish belief is written into the first pages of the book of Genesis: all of us are made in the very image and likeness of God. In other words, in our deepest reality, there abides the character and spirit of God.

This is one extraordinary belief. It suggests that within ourselves we carry divine potential—an endless capacity to love, a bottomless well of forgiveness, compassion, and generosity. Jesus held no doubt about our capacity to let this divine spirit loose in our lives: "'Be compassionate just as your Father is compassionate'" (Luke 6:36). And again, when asked by Peter how often one could be expected to forgive another, Jesus answered with the startling ideal "'Not seven, I tell you, but seventy-seven times'" (Matthew 18:22).

In Jewish idiom, this meant unceasingly. Our capacity to forgive is limitless. In his own prayer we ask God to forgive us our faults just as we forgive those of others. God's and our capacities to forgive are not different.

Therefore, it should not surprise us that in this encounter with the paralyzed man, Jesus took upon himself the authority of that divine core within all human beings, and he gave it voice by forgiving sin in God's name. To have the courage and greatness of heart to forgive in God's name is a sacred, human activity.

To believe this is one thing. To act upon it is another. For Jesus, to be game enough to publicly take this step required personal courage and a comfortableness with God that seemed shocking and brazen to many of his contemporaries. The whole issue turns on how a person understands God. Understanding is itself dependent upon one's experience.

No wonder they said he blasphemed. No wonder the people standing there were astounded. There was much, much more going on here than a simple physical cure.

Jesus saw this as an issue of justice. Presumptions of sin are an injustice both to the person concerned and also to God. Jesus was driven by a sense of justice. To protect the self-esteem and dignity of the paralyzed man as well as to defend the God he knew, Jesus chose the dangerous path of publicly speaking with God's authority.

In so doing, he was taking on the religious culture of his day at one of its deepest levels. This was simply part of the commitment Jesus had made at baptism.

What an extraordinary inner freedom he must have possessed.

Nor is there any competitiveness in him. Notice the care with which Mark said that Jesus noticed the faith and loyalty of the sick man's friends. How graciously Jesus attributed the forgiveness to *them*. It was *their* faith that convinced him of the absence of sin. Their goodness persuaded him of their friend's inner goodness: "seeing *their* faith, Jesus said...."

This happens so frequently in the gospels. Jesus never allowed himself to be distracted by the sorts of things that tend to fascinate us: he was always on the lookout for the *goodness, looking to name the sacredness and faith* that existed in those he met. Jesus would have to be the one person in history most oriented toward "goodness." He instinctively noticed goodness and love. "*Your* faith has saved you!" or "*your* faith has made you whole" are comments that occur frequently in the gospels. It's the same here: he could not restrain himself from commenting on the faith and courageous loyalty of the paralyzed man's few friends. Jesus never seems to have thought of himself as the only one possessed by God's graciousness. He noticed—and commented upon—God's presence beyond himself. No narrow mind here! It's no wonder people were amazed.

This was really the miracle at which they marveled. It was as easy for "a human one" to forgive sin in the name of God as it was to invite a paralyzed person to stand and walk free again.

They had never seen anything like this. In their wildest dreams they had never imagined a person could act and speak with such poise and freedom. It had been a long time since they had seen anyone "take on" the authorities so calmly and effectively. Here he was, one like themselves, and fighting on their behalf against the crushing religious system—saying the things that none of them dared believe could be said. No wonder they were saying to one another, "'We have never seen anything like this.'"

For Prayer

This encounter has changed Jesus. Something has been freed up in him and come into words for the first time. Today, in that crowd, he acted out for the first time something of his deeper belief about the God he has come to know. The God he "spoke for" today was the God of his mother and father—the God of his ancestors whose stories he loves so passionately.

This God is very close to all of us, and on this day Jesus knows that he gave voice to a sacred presence in life—knows that he spoke words of forgiveness in God's name. And God confirmed his daring to do so by curing the paralysis of the one Jesus blessed.

The questions must rise reverently in his mind while at prayer: "Who are you, my God? Where are you, my God? Is the mystery of your presence so close to us?"

Allow yourself to sense the reverence and mystery rising in the heart of Jesus as he contemplates the awesome truth of what occurred that day.

For Discussion

- If this divine potential lies within all of us, what does this realization do to the way you look at others?
- What then, in these terms of divine potential, is the mission of the Church? The mission of your local parish? Is it our task to bring to our world and its people something they don't possess, or is it to uncover and confirm a goodness already present?

5
Into Fire

Another time he went into the *synagogue,* and there was a man present whose hand was withered. And *they were watching him* to see if he would cure him *on the Sabbath day,* hoping for *something to charge him with.* He said to the man with the withered hand, "Get up and stand *in the middle!*" Then he said to them, "Is it permitted on the Sabbath day to do good, or to do evil; to save life, or to kill?" But *they said nothing.* Then he looked *angrily* round at them, *grieved to find them so obstinate,* and said to the man, "Stretch out your hand." He stretched it out and his hand was restored. The *Pharisees* went out and began at once to plot with the *Herodians* against him, *discussing how to destroy him.*

Mark 3:1–6 (emphasis added)

THE SYMBOLISM OF this story is powerful. Mark told us more in this story than might at first appear. It is not simply about a marvelous cure that Jesus performed, as if the power to heal proved he was God. In fact, it has almost nothing to do with this "miraculous" understanding we had as children. There was a miracle here, right enough. Something happened in this story that was extraordinary, amazing, and wonderful. But the miracle described here is dangerously closer to our daily experience than the healing of an arthritic hand. This is a story about baptism and commitment to justice.

Mark saw this encounter as pretty typical of what Jesus did in his public ministry. It portrays the sort of person Jesus was and the kind of values for which he was prepared to live dangerously—even to die—if necessary. He took a stand for human dignity and common sense, inner freedom. It is a story about *true* religion.

The society in which Jesus lived was religiously driven. He challenged attitudes and structures that were unjust to the poor, the little people, and the disadvantaged. He saw how injustice hardened the hearts of *everybody*. Having committed himself to correcting such injustice, he had no choice but to challenge head-on the religious authorities of his day. He had to take them on right in their own territory and on their own terms. His love for the truly sacred—whether in the poor or in the powerful—drove him to name in public and with stinging ferocity those issues within Jewish society that crucified and buried the poor, whether in the name of *God* or *tradition* or *law*.

Note the situation of the story. It happened in a synagogue and on the Sabbath—in the sacred space and in sacred time. Mark told us that Jesus took his challenge right into the very heart of Judaism, penetrating even into those reserved areas that nobody had permission to question openly. Jesus was a commoner; it was out of bounds to question synagogue and Sabbath and custom. Such things were none of his business, but the preserve of the hierarchy, who saw themselves as "sacred" people. They were the guardians and interpreters of Judaism. Tradition was their territory, and the Sabbath was their domain.

Yet Jesus took them on right in their sacred space. He decided to confront their manipulation of the sacred Sabbath.

For they were manipulative. They were being dishonest. They were betraying their deeper selves and their own sense of the sacred; *they* were the ones violating synagogue and Sabbath by using them as an entrapment to diminish Jesus. They were playing games with God. Jesus could tolerate neither the insult to the God he knew nor the diminishment they were inflicting on themselves by so doing. He took them on. If they wanted a fight, then so be it!

Let it happen in broad daylight for all to see: "He said to the man with the withered hand, 'Get up and stand in the middle!'"

Notice how Jesus did not set out to diminish the Pharisees in the confrontation. It was not his way to diminish anyone. He felt deeply for what they were doing to themselves by their subterfuge. He realized that *they* were the first victims of such dishonesty—that it was the divine potential within themselves that was being trashed. In compassion he appealed to their better selves. He questioned them on issues of life and death, good and evil, offering them a way out of the public impasse they had initiated. His question gave them the chance of gracious retreat. They could choose to answer in such a way that their awareness of justice and their love for truth would be evident to all. They could opt for life, not death, and declare their option publicly. He invited them to think more deeply before compromising themselves completely.

But they had nothing to say. They would not even consider that they had something to learn. Their hearts could not admit even the possibility that they were acting unjustly. It was this pigheaded stupidity that grieved Jesus deeply—for he loved them. Yet their capacity to violate and abuse others (this poor man with the withered hand) and to burden ordinary people with their presumed authority angered him beyond words. They chose to stand silent; Jesus was stung into dangerous action.

He took it upon himself to act with the authority they could not summon—the authority of God. This synagogue was God's place and this Sabbath God's day—so let the God of life and justice take possession of the moment! The courage of God, whose image he carried deep in his being, was roused to action: Enough of using this poor, disfigured man! Enough of this abuse of so-called sacred power! Enough of the charade that passed for religion! Enough of making burdens for the people! Time to stand and speak one's truth...

"'Stretch out your hand.'"

Jesus affronted their power. Their self-identity had become so bound up with their position within the structure that to challenge their interpretation of things was to challenge their very persons. There was no repentance in them, no learning. Instead of deeper love, they chose deeper violence. Incapable of the humility that alone makes conversion possible, they would now compromise themselves completely. He would pay for their loss of face! They began negotiations with the Herodian party for his murder.

Commentators tell us that the Herodians and the Pharisees were usually bitter rivals—but look how prepared they were to go down even *that* path rather than reconsider the direction of their lives. Prestige had corrupted their inner honesty—they were unable to turn their lives around. Having lost their inner freedom, they had lost all sense of themselves as made in the likeness and image of God's own goodness. The Spirit could not reach them.

This is a story about the baptism Jesus lived. He was publicly committed to the justice of God. No longer could he *not* live the image in which he was born—into which all of us are born. He would tolerate no denial of that image in any of us, for it alone gives us our deepest dignity and meaning. This was the source of the belief Jesus had in people. For him, the potential of God lay in all of us. To miss this was "to sin" against the Spirit. This belief liberated him, enthused others, and communicated itself like fire in stubble.

No human institution—synagogue or Sabbath, no matter how sacred—stands immune to the judgment of such fire.

For Prayer

Jesus was deeply grieved at the Pharisees' hardness of heart and at what they were doing to themselves, let alone to others. We must not miss his compassion for these men.

Imagine in your mind's eye that it is the evening of that same day and Jesus is at prayer alone. He is letting the memory of the morning pass again through his heart. Sense in your own quiet way how deep is his grief for those Pharisees, how deeply he loves them despite their blindness and stupidity. Will he not be praying on their behalf, "'Father, forgive them; they do not know what they are doing'" (Luke 23:34)?

Hear him ask himself whether, for their sakes as well, he could have handled things better that morning. Ask the Spirit to help you "tune in" to what is happening in his heart and mind. Let yourself get inside his skin, as it were; inside his mind and heart.

For Discussion

- Many suggest that one of the most important issues facing the Church today is that of authority. It is certainly of utmost importance to speak about this matter in ways that do not diminish the persons involved—for that would be to betray the very justice in which Jesus lived.
- Why might it be that Catholics generally find it difficult to discuss authority in loving and calm ways? Just as importantly, why might it be that institutional authority has become such a major issue for us? Are there echoes in the story above that remind you of your experience in the Church?

    In discussing, keep referring to the authority Jesus took in the story above. What was driving him? What drives us?
- What is the important role of institutional authority in a Church? How should our personal authority relate to it? What implications do you see for us in this story?

6
Covering for Zacchaeus

He entered Jericho and was going through the town and suddenly a man whose name was Zacchaeus made his appearance; he was one of the *senior tax collectors* and a *wealthy* man. *He kept trying to see which Jesus was,* but he was too short and could not see him for the crowd; so he ran ahead and *climbed a sycamore tree* to catch a glimpse of Jesus who was to pass that way. When Jesus reached the spot he looked up and *spoke* to him, "Zacchaeus, come down. Hurry, because I am to stay at your house today." And he hurried down and welcomed him joyfully. They all complained when they saw what was happening. "He has gone to stay at a sinner's house," they said. But Zacchaeus *stood his ground* and said to the Lord, "Look, sir, I am going to give half my property to the poor, and if I have cheated anybody I will pay him back four times the amount." And Jesus said to him, "Today *salvation has come* to this house, because this man too is a *son of Abraham;* for the Son of man has come to seek out and save what was lost."

Luke 19:1–10 (emphasis added)

THIS IS A REVEALING STORY, well known to anyone trying to teach the sacrament of reconciliation. The problem that teachers find with this story is that nowhere did Jesus actually forgive Zacchaeus' sin—at least, not in terms that we would normally recognize as forgiveness.

The surprise is, of course, that there was more "sin" around in this story than what dear Zacchaeus admitted to. And a second surprise is that Jesus wasn't the only person bestowing forgiveness. To understand what I mean, we must fully appreciate the situation in which Zacchaeus found himself.

All who volunteered—or were forced—into collecting taxes for the Roman administration were treated as traitors by the Jewish people—worse than nonpersons. They were hated, despised, and deeply alienated from society.

Zacchaeus was a "senior" tax collector. His percentage, or coverage, would have been high. He was known as a "wealthy" man, and it was *Jewish* wealth that he had accumulated! It is safe to presume that he would have been shunned in public. His short physical stature was in sharp contrast to the apparent size of both his ego and his bank balance.

Zacchaeus did not know Jesus. The story indicates that they had never previously met, and Zacchaeus, curious to know "what kind of man Jesus was," joined the crowd that day. It was not a crowd in which he was at home. He was shunted to the back. His stature prevented his seeing Jesus.

Still, caught up in the moment and using his head, he hurried further along the street and, momentarily shedding his public reserve, hoisted himself like the boy he once had been into a roadside tree to enjoy the passing spectacle.

Reality abruptly caught up with Zacchaeus. He was noticed, not only by the unfriendly crowd, but also by Jesus. He suddenly found himself the center of unwanted attention: exposed, literally "out on a limb" and up a tree. His position was ridiculous, and the crowd who had always wanted to "give it" to him were suddenly in a position to do so. Like laundry on a clothesline, Zacchaeus was on view.

Jesus immediately sensed his predicament and how it had come about. He sensed the mood and judgment of the crowd and realized how fragile the moment had become for Zacchaeus. So Jesus decided to "cover" for him—he spoke to him as if to a longstanding friend: "Zacchaeus! Nice to see you again! What a surprise! Remember *(wink)* that I've an invitation to stay with you today!" (author's paraphrase).

The "forgiveness" lay in Jesus' whole attitude to people. He refused to play the judgmental games of society. He knew that such judgment would shred a person's inner dignity. His judgment, on the contrary, was that all are sacred. In the beautifully Jewish mind of Jesus, justice demanded that the inner sacredness of each person be noticed, confirmed, and thereby extended. He would not tolerate the dismissive mind. He would not act in ways that alienated, categorized, or cornered people or in ways that diminished them. As a public person caught in a compromising situation, Zacchaeus was right on the edge of such dangerous ridicule— and Jesus immediately helped him.

Zacchaeus recognized the rope Jesus was throwing him. He was being offered a gracious exit from his predicament. Old hand that he was when it came to subterfuge, he responded warmly to Jesus and hurried down to welcome him like an old friend. The crowd was disarmed by this unexpected familiarity. Zacchaeus' dignity was maintained—and in public. Jesus had given him room to move. The person (even beneath the role of tax-man) was far too important for Jesus to allow his humiliation. Jesus provided the opportunity that Zacchaeus took with both hands. The crowd was thunderstruck: far from being "out on a limb" as they had supposed, Zacchaeus actually *knew* this Jesus!

Zacchaeus responded to Jesus' invitation with an equal generosity. If Jesus had been courageous, so would he be. If Jesus could be big-hearted, so could Zacchaeus. If Jesus had convictions about a person's inner goodness, so did he. Zacchaeus realized his better self. He was at heart a man of justice. There was a generous side to Zacchaeus that others did not even suspect, and he now showed unusual courage—and humility—by placing these deeper qualities in public view. During the meal he uncovered his better self, he stood up to be counted—just as Jesus had done under the tree. Jesus had put some ginger into Zacchaeus!

How did Zacchaeus stand up to be counted? First, he showed

his unqualified appreciation by giving Jesus the honor of his home. He "went public" and allied himself with this unusual man, Jesus—despite what people might say.

Notice the lovely phrase Mark used: he "stood his ground." This phrase is crucial for understanding the whole story.

It was *his* ground on which Zacchaeus stood; it was *his* dignity that he exercised; it was *his own* potential that was realized. His capacity to be recklessly generous lay already within himself. Jesus hadn't put it there—it had always been there. Jesus had simply shown Zacchaeus the potential of which the human heart is capable. Zacchaeus stepped into that potential thoughtfully and courageously.

His gratitude for how Jesus "saved" him at the tree turned into a similar generosity. He would donate half his possessions to the poor (for Zacchaeus now knew what it was like to be "out on a limb" and poor himself). Having been himself desperate for largess, he would not deny that same largess to others. If anyone had a legitimate financial complaint, he would honor that fourfold. The wellsprings of God-like justice were flowing in Zacchaeus. If possible, he would outdo even this Jesus in generosity and justice. He "stood his ground" with pride.

This interaction was not lost on Jesus. He was overwhelmed by what he was witnessing in Zacchaeus. This was salvation alive! This was the justice Jesus recognized. This was the kingdom indeed! It was as if Jesus were commenting for all to hear, "'...salvation has come to this house....'"

There is no suggestion here that Jesus saw himself as having introduced salvation to the home of Zacchaeus. It resided there already. It was Jesus who was touched by the wonder of what was occurring before his eyes. Delighted with what he saw, Jesus was growing as well. The goodness and generosity that Zacchaeus had displayed was utter covenant; this was what it meant to be Jewish. This was mainstream faith, and Jesus could not restrain from exclaiming, "'...this man too is a son of Abraham....'" No more gracious compliment could have been handed to Zacchaeus—and given in public: he, a tax-collector, was a *true son* of Abraham, no longer alienated or marginalized. The harsh judgment of people was revoked, and in front of the very people among whom it mattered. Zacchaeus was fully and fundamentally reinstated to his God-given dignity. He had become reconciled once more with his deepest truth. This was truly a lesson in reconciliation for all involved.

It had all stemmed from the attitude of Jesus. He was of a mind never to judge a person into diminishment. Rather, Jesus had this habitual perception of a person's deeper goodness. He operated out of a conviction that a person's deepest heart is shaped on that of the God he knew, and that all a person ultimately needs is the encouragement to take hold of that divine potential. It seems to have been the mission of Jesus to reconcile us to the divine potential we carry. It is forgiveness, in a way, for it depends totally on how we forgive one another the poor and immature ways we attempt to live our God-given capacities. It depends on our not "missing the point" of our own and other's lives.

So we can ask ourselves, what does forgiveness actually mean? Jesus possessed a mind that "gave way" for another to grow. Such "giving-for" another was the ground and source of his whole ministry. This was education in its true sense: to lead a person out into something more broad and freeing (in Latin, *educare* means "to lead out"). All honest education involves the releasing of a person's deepest, God-given potential.

This is also the meaning of reconciliation: to "come home" to one's true self; to be "at home" with that image and likeness of God in which all of us are made. Surely, a primary aspect of reconciliation involves coming to terms with one's true self.

For Prayer

All of us carry something of Zacchaeus in our lives. We carry memories that if known would expose the hollowness of who we like to think we are in the eyes of others. In short, we struggle.

Let the realization of how much of a struggler you are come home to you. Let it sit comfortably upon you for some quiet moments. In the privacy of your own heart, let yourself be real to yourself.

Then, while thus aware of your humanness, of the ways you have lived "up a tree" in life, let your mind's eye catch the face of Jesus looking up at you, just as he caught the knowing eye of Zacchaeus in this story. Let Jesus look at you with the same conspiratorial intimacy.

Let yourself become aware of what Jesus sees in you, deep within you. What is it that Jesus values in you? What does he admire in you?

For Discussion

- Working from this story, what do you think it means to have a reconciling mind like Jesus? Discuss what you believe was the basis for his way of perceiving people like Zacchaeus.

- *To be reconciled to our deepest potential.* Discuss what this might mean to people today. If this is one fundamental aspect of reconciliation, what might be some other implications for our lives as a staff, parish, or group?

7
Fighting for the Woman

One of the Pharisees invited him [Jesus] to a meal. When he arrived at the Pharisee's house and took his place at table, suddenly a woman came in, *who had a bad name in the town.* She had heard he was dining with the Pharisee and had brought with her an alabaster jar of ointment. She waited behind him at his feet, weeping, and her tears fell on his feet, and she wiped them away with her hair; then she covered his feet with kisses and anointed them with ointment.

When the Pharisee who had invited him saw this, he said to *himself,* "If this man were a prophet, he would know who this woman is and *what sort of person it is who is touching him and what a bad name she has.*" Then Jesus took him up and said, "Simon, I have something to say to you." He replied, "Say on, Master." "There was once a creditor who had two men in his debt; one owed him five hundred denarii, the other fifty. They were unable to pay, so he let them both off. Which of them will love him more?" Simon answered, "The one who was let off more, I suppose." Jesus said, "You are right."

Then he turned to the woman and said to Simon, "You see this woman? I came into your house, and you poured no water over my feet, but she has poured out her tears over my feet and wiped them away with her hair. You gave me no kiss, but she has been covering my feet with kisses ever since I came in. You did not anoint my head with oil, but she has anointed my feet with ointment. For this reason I tell you that her sins, many as they are, have been forgiven her, *because she has shown such great love.* It is someone who is forgiven little who shows little love." Then he said to her, *"Your sins are forgiven."* Those who were with him at table began to say to themselves, "Who is this man, that even forgives sins?" But he said to the woman, "Your faith has saved you; go in peace."

Luke 7:36–50 (emphasis added)

WE ALREADY APPRECIATE that, in the time of Jesus, women were second-class citizens. It was not customary even to speak to them in public.

The woman of this story is a well-recognized prostitute. Luke told us that she was well known for her "bad name." Probably her manner of dressing declared her profession and livelihood. She was a sinner. Therefore, she was outcast and beyond the pale to God's good people. To be seen speaking in public with any man was tantamount to admitting that some intimacy existed between them. She was a nonperson, shunned by society.

All the more amazing, then, that she displayed such strength of character. She not only dared to walk the street in broad daylight—everyone knowing her well—but she presumed to gate-crash the home and meal of a leading Pharisee. It's worth stopping for a moment to consider the self-possession and courage that this demanded.

She was a strong woman, not afraid of what people might think of her. Apparently, her concern for public esteem had long since gone. She was desperate, and in that sense, she couldn't have cared less for the opinions of others. In gate-crashing this occasion, she risked whatever she had left in terms of being acceptable. It was a gesture of all or nothing—born out of a desperate longing to be accepted by someone for who she was. It was a gesture carried through with personal poise and calm self-possession. Jesus noted it well.

She simply placed herself at the feet of Jesus, quietly weeping. Awkwardly, she removed her fallen tears with her hair. She kissed his feet in respect. More than this, she had come prepared with a jar of welcoming-ointment to honor this man whom she considered to be deserving of the most profound recognition—and she knew what it was to be hungry for recognition. She had heard of him. What she had heard had earned her deepest respect. She quietly anointed his feet. No words. No fuss. No interruption to the meal. She simply went about what she had come to do.

It is not difficult to imagine what Simon the Pharisee thought about all this carrying-on. Even were it not written all over Simon's face, Jesus was Jewish enough to know the likely reactions to such a woman's presence. Interestingly, Simon lacked the courage to voice his thoughts in the presence of Jesus. As so often in gospel stories, the unloving reaction was kept to the privacy of the mind, and the bias toward judgment was masked by silence. It was a silence that someone had to break. Unafraid to speak *his* mind, Jesus quietly moved toward the unspoken issue with a seemingly harmless story.

Jesus then turned toward the woman and spoke on her behalf. Publicly, he placed the best possible construction on her clumsy, unconventional actions. His words ennobled her. He showed deep appreciation for what she had done. He responded to her love, describing her as someone gracious and hospitable. The kindness of his words was not lost on her.

The woman had risked everything in entering the house. It was a courage that Jesus rose to match. If she could risk so much, then in her defense so would he. For Jesus, she embodied the goodness and dignified respect for others about which the whole covenant with God turned. She embodied the kingdom. There was no way he could do anything but warm to her in that moment.

The risk she took was immense. The risk that Jesus now took on her behalf was even more so.

Her lifestyle marked her as sinner and prostitute. There was no doubt about her sin. The facts were there to be seen. The jury was in on this one. And in the face of it all, despite every shred of evidence to the contrary, Jesus read her status with God through the lens of her capacity for graciousness.

If a person could do something so gracious, so thoughtful, so loving, and so courageous, then she could not be far wide of the mark in her life! Her "sin," whatever it was, must already have been gone. Jesus was prepared to match her courage and to declare quite publicly that she was "forgiven."

What does *forgiven* mean? The Greek word used by Luke means "to have something dismissed, sent away, or tossed aside." It's as if Jesus were saying, "Your sin is gone…you are no longer in that condition people call sin. Your love and graciousness is far too obvious for that to be still true."

Given the public price she had had to pay for "having a bad name," nothing more liberating could have been said to her. For someone to declare so publicly that she was not a sinner, that was one thing. But for that same person to treat her as normal, as having dignity and respect—this was another thing entirely. She had been declared wholesome. She could walk from this encounter with her head held high and refuse to believe any longer the lie that she was worthless.

No wonder the Church would eventually come to call such an experience "salvation," or "redemption," or "liberation."

Let's not underestimate the courage of Jesus in uttering, as a layperson, the forbidden words "Your sins are forgiven."

These were words reserved to God and to the "holy men" of the day. And here was Jesus, a commoner and layperson, daring to take to himself this "reserved" authority! In his own heart he believed it was possible, so he now committed himself to act on that belief—to give utterance to the unutterable.

It was for *her* sake that he acted. It was as if this one woman's courage and kindness freed something in Jesus that he would otherwise never have dared face. We can forgive one another's sins—this was his conviction. He stepped beyond caution and put his conviction on the line. This was the kingdom indeed. This was very good news.

Those who witnessed this assault on religious convention became nervous about what was occurring: "Who does he think he is? Only God can forgive sins! What's really going on here?" (author's paraphrase). Notice again how carefully they kept such dangerous thoughts "to themselves." The implications for growth and for faith are explosive.

During this momentary but profound interaction with the woman, Jesus grew immensely. He had no doubts about where the Spirit he experienced in that moment had originated. He named its location before the woman had time to depart. There was no doubting it, so let there be no mistake: "'*Your* faith has saved you; go in peace'" (emphasis added). Jesus attributed Spirit to the woman— not to himself. Jesus had not "saved" her. It was the Spirit of God emerging from the woman's own depths that had "saved" her. This final word of affirmation from Jesus sealed her conviction that she was again one of the blessed people of God. Among God's people she was no alien, no stranger; she was no longer different, no longer an intruder on ground reserved for "the chosen." Jesus gave her the space in which to walk tall and free. He was so careful to comment publicly before she left that his capacity to respond so graciously had been triggered by the Spirit within *her*. He knew that he had received something of great value from her long before he returned the compliment in this divine conversation.

For Prayer

Imagine that it is later that afternoon, perhaps close to sundown. Jesus has found some solitude. He is still affected by the woman whom he met that morning. He is still in awe of her courage, her determination, and her graciousness. He is still deeply touched.

Gently imagine what is going through his mind's eye as he allows himself to remember her from that morning. Let yourself begin to notice what feelings are going through his heart as he remembers her so clearly and with such pleasure and admiration. Let him recall in his mind's eye how the morning unfolded so surprisingly. As you do this, notice what is occurring in your own feelings.

For Discussion

- This woman, in her courage and desperation, released in Jesus a responding courage and an authority to dare do what he would otherwise not have done. In other words, Jesus grew in this encounter.

- In the language of the New Testament, the word *sin* basically means "to miss the point." This woman was considered by all to have missed the point about God's law— she was known as "a sinner."

  Jesus on the other hand, seemed to think that there was much more "missing the point" going on than people were prepared to notice or admit. To those who came to know him well, Jesus himself was remarkable in that he seemed never to "miss the point" of his life (see Hebrews 4:15).

  Using this story as data, what do you believe Jesus thought *was* the point of it all? What was his life about?

- What do these considerations do to your sense of sin? What is happening in your heart as we ponder these sacred issues? What are the implications for us?

8

Past Horizons That I Know

Jesus left that place and withdrew to the region of Tyre and Sidon. And suddenly out came a *Canaanite woman from that district* and started shouting, "Lord, *Son of David*, take pity on me. My daughter is tormented by a devil." *But he said not a word in answer to her.* And his disciples went and pleaded with him, saying, "Give her what she wants, because she keeps shouting after us." He said in reply, "I was sent only to the lost sheep of the *House* of *Israel*." But the woman had come up and was bowing low before him. "Lord," she said, "help me." He replied, "It is not fair to take the children's food and throw it to *little dogs*." She retorted, "Ah yes, Lord; but *even little dogs* eat the scraps that fall from their masters' table." Then Jesus answered her, "Woman, *you have great faith*. Let your desire be granted." And from that moment her daughter was well again.

Matthew 15:21–28 (emphasis added)

THIS IS A MARVELOUS story of how Jesus grew in understanding himself. In a way that perhaps startles us, it captures an amazing truth that Jesus grew and matured and that his mind developed as he did so. Luke expressed the same thing in the first chapters of his gospel: "And Jesus increased in wisdom, in stature, and in favour with God and with people" (Luke 2:52).

This passage clearly indicates the growth process of Jesus' mind and heart. He was like us. As a child he thought like a child. His mind was like ours. He matured and developed as we do. Allowing the truth of this to make an impact on our minds and hearts takes us into the mystery of it all. Who was he?

The gospels are filled with data that indicate how he developed in understanding himself and his life. This story of the Canaanite woman is one such story. Jesus had to "listen" to life and profit from that daily experience—just as we do. He had to pay close attention to what occurred from day to day in his life if he was to stay faithful to the movements of God. He had to be attentive and learn how to notice. He had to make choices between paths that would diminish him and roads that would enlarge him. In this sense, his life was a constant dance with God.

Let us look at the story in detail. He and his disciples were in need of time for themselves. They crossed the border into non-Jewish territory, near the seaside towns of Tyre and Sidon. This would be the southern part of Lebanon today. Jewish settlers lived in the region, but the population was mostly non-Jewish. The Canaanite woman was one of these.

We know two things about her: she had heard something about Jesus' reputation, and she loved her daughter deeply. We also know that it wasn't the done thing for a woman to accost a strange man in public (let alone a Jewish man), but in her desperation and love she threw caution to the winds.

She treated Jesus with utmost respect, using the title "Lord" and calling him a "Son of David." She was showing respect for his Jewish roots. But the fact that he was male, Jewish, and from an entirely different culture would not prevent her desperate appeal on behalf of her daughter.

It can horrify us to realize that Jesus simply ignored her. He couldn't even bring himself to speak to her. And remember, back in his own culture, this was the man who took the courageous initiative in breaking the silence in which society enclosed its women. It was extraordinary behavior on his part to answer her "not a word"!

The only possible explanation for his attitude becomes evident as the story unfolds. She was not Jewish, and Jesus would have nothing to do with her—plead as she might! At this period of his life, evidently his understanding was that he was meant for his own people. The mission he saw for himself had nothing to do with anyone beyond Judaism. He was Jewish. His concern was Judaism.

It is difficult for us to admit such tunnel vision on the part of Jesus: it disturbs our fantasies of who he was. Yet the data of the story are clear and compelling.

The disciples made the first move, more out of annoyance than any genuine sense of compassion. Like Jesus, they also had little commitment to a foreigner—yet she was becoming too much of a nuisance to ignore. In exasperation, they begged Jesus to do something—for their sakes, not for hers.

Jesus tried to justify himself to his disciples. She was not Jewish. She was none of his business. By this time, however, the woman was within earshot, and whether Jesus liked it or not, she would engage him, make him at least talk directly to her—even if she had to beg.

She did so, throwing herself at his feet. She could no longer be avoided. This time Jesus spoke directly to her, but his words were harsh and dismissive—tantamount to calling her a dog. He obviously could not see his way clearly. He was caught between the demands of his Jewish culture and a desperate woman. This was an experience totally new to him—being approached by someone who did not fit his Jewish experience. She had caught him unaware. He was not sure of himself, not sure of the next step. But he was open to dialogue now, which was more than he had been prepared to undertake a few minutes previously. Jesus was searching for truth because the territory was suddenly unfamiliar.

It was *her* courage and commitment that opened the way for him.

She took his jibe about dogs; for the sake of her daughter she would wear that. She accepted his contention that the Jews were God's people. But driven by love, she stepped into the truth of her condition before him. It was a love Jesus noticed. Suddenly, she was coming to embody realities that Jesus could recognize: *his* eyes were opened and he *saw*—as if for the first time—the courage, the faith, and the single-minded love of this extraordinary woman at his feet. He could not help himself saying, "'Woman, you have great faith.'"

This woman, a complete stranger, had succeeded in educating Jesus into a deeper truth about himself. In this encounter Jesus was humbled. In this encounter Jesus grew, and the horizons of his mind broadened far beyond Judaism.

Could there be a story in the gospels more filled with hope for us than this delightful episode? No wonder the early Church treasured such a gospel story. Within a few years of Jesus' death we witness the whole Jerusalem Church debating this very issue: should the Church stay Jewish in its culture, or should it be big enough to broaden its horizons to include the cultures of others?

In this story Jesus was quite aware of who was educating whom. He knew that he was on the receiving end of this interaction. He left this woman in no doubt that it was *her* faith that effected the cure of her daughter. If he had turned a corner in his own mind and come to a new understanding of his life, then it was this simple and determined woman who had led him there.

For Prayer

This encounter had an enormous impact on Jesus. He would have pondered over it many times—certainly at the end of that particularly eventful day. It had begun as such an ordinary day, but it had ended with his seeing his life from a totally different perspective. The experience would have awed him.

Sense him sitting in stillness at day's end, pondering the wonder of how easily and unexpectedly God has broken again into his life. How easy it would have been to have missed that divine moment of insight! Sense the reverence in Jesus' heart for this God who so delicately catches him off guard and then swoops to enlighten him. Catch a sense of how Jesus would appreciate the playfulness and tenderness of such a Father.

For Discussion

- The capacity to grow and to learn throughout life is one of the most sacred and divine qualities we possess.

  Discuss the truth of this in terms of your experience.
- "To have is to change, and to be perfect is to have changed often" (John Henry Newman).

  Discuss the truth of this in relation to Jesus.

9
Out of Chaos, Courage

And at once he made his disciples get into the boat and go on ahead to the other side near Bethsaida, while he himself sent the crowd away. After saying good-bye to them *he went off into the hills to pray.* When evening came, the boat was far out on the sea, and he was alone on the land. He could see that they were hard pressed in their rowing, for *the wind was against them;* and about the *fourth* watch of the night he came towards them, walking on the sea. He was going to pass them by, but when they saw him *walking on the sea* they thought it was a ghost and cried out; for they had all seen him and were terrified. But at once he spoke to them and said, *"Courage! It's me! Don't be afraid."* Then he got into the boat with them and the wind dropped. They were utterly and completely dumbfounded, because *they had not seen what the miracle of the loaves meant;* their minds were closed.

Mark 6:45–52 (emphasis added)

WHEN I WAS A CHILD, this scene proved to me that Jesus was God. He could walk on water. He could do anything he wished.

People still joke about those who can "walk on water." It is usually meant to indicate how such people consider themselves a cut above the rest of us! Yet when we read the story carefully, we wonder how such a serious misunderstanding of the story could have happened.

Two mistakes can be made about this story: the first is that we try to make sense of it as an isolated story, without reading carefully the pieces of the gospel that lead up to it. Second, we fail to read it *as a story* and presume that it describes, literally, what must have occurred on one stormy night of Jesus' life.

I will treat it here as a story. It may, of course, have actually happened. But I suggest that its reality is not the point. Whether it happened or not, Mark made it into a delightfully intelligent commentary on our human condition and on the Spirit of God who moves among us. In other words, there is a truth he was trying to express about God, about life, and about the depths of courage that lie in all of us. To do this in an easily memorized way, Mark used the waters of the lake, a storm, strong winds, and the events that led up to this "night" in the life of Jesus. These events are most important.

Three experiences precede this story of Jesus walking on water. They are all found in chapter 6 of Mark's Gospel (or a little more graphically, in chapter 14 of Matthew). It is worth taking time to see what they are, for they provide the setting for the story we are considering.

1. Jesus, realizing the immensity of the task he had undertaken, sent his apostles out to the townships to cover the ground more quickly. He sent them on mission. They set out to do what he had been doing.

2. King Herod began to take an interest in Jesus and in what he was doing. This Herod had killed John the Baptist, and some silly people were beginning to suggest that Jesus was John the Baptist back from the dead. The story was then told of how John had died. His death was a frightening obscenity to any God-loving Jew. John had died for no good reason: Herod had even decided not to kill him because he was afraid of the people's reaction, but then felt caught by big-mouth promises made while drunk. In fact, Herod was said to have been "deeply distressed" when faced with the sad consequences of his words. John's life was cut short.

This great and profound man was murdered on the merest whim. It was difficult to handle such wastage of life.

Even more, John was mutilated. For a Jew, this was an obscenity. Enemies were sometimes mutilated to prevent their entering the next life as well. Could this be John's shocking fate? God's holy person? Where was God and justice in all this?

Notice how impersonal the language became once John was so killed: they carried "the head" on a dish and gave "it" to the girl who gave "it" to her mother. His disciples took "his body" and laid "it" in a tomb. It's as if, with his mutilation, John's person had somehow ceased to be.

3. In deep grief at this news, Jesus and his disciples crossed the lake to find time and space for themselves in the desert. To their dismay, a large crowd was waiting for them. Jesus sidelined his own urgent needs and gave himself to them. As evening fell, even the disciples became concerned for the crowd, wondering how to feed them. Jesus challenged them to give the crowd their own food, entirely.

The disciples found these three events deeply disturbing. Jesus had sent them on mission, and immediately Mark painted a picture of what the same mission had cost John. They needed time for themselves but were immediately faced with the challenge to give away "all they have" so that others might be fed. The lesson was directed at the disciples: this was what it meant to follow Jesus; this was what it meant to be baptized into his mission. Jesus sent the crowds away while the apostles headed homeward in the boat.

The symbols in this story are momentous. Let us stay with them for a little while, treating the images mentioned as symbolic of all our lives. It is not important whether it happened like this or not. Jesus was shocked by John's death. People had already begun to call Jesus a prophet too. The cost of living for God's kingdom and standing up for justice were sheeted home to Jesus when he was faced with John's murder. He needed to make sense of these events; he needed time to pray and to come to terms with what was happening. He was in grief over John whom he loved. He was frightened by what had happened.

Yet he was also torn by the need to feed the hungry crowds with truth and with his life. When he saw the waiting crowd, Jesus had to give again. Like the apostles faced with a hungry crowd, he gave them all he had as a teacher. When this extraordinary day was over he had to pray. He went alone into the hills in the early evening.

How Jesus prayed that night is hidden from us. But the outcome of those hours alone in the hills becomes clear from what followed. For one thing, he prayed for a long time: from "when evening came" until "the fourth watch of the night" (sometime around three in the morning). It was a long night.

The apostles were rowing across *the waters,* and *the wind* was against them.

In Jewish culture, deep waters symbolized all that was chaotic in life. The deeps were the abode of evil spirits. Right back into the Genesis stories of creation, it was the Spirit of God that hovered *over* the waters, those primeval, restless, unformed realities that contained monsters and death. It was upon "the waters" that the apostles were rowing. John's murder, the cost of sharing the mission of Jesus, the need to give everything they possessed to the hungry crowds—these were the harsh realities that the apostles were facing. This was what it meant to follow Jesus. This was "the chaos" upon which they were rowing for their lives.

And the *wind* was against them. Christians know well what *the wind* symbolizes—the Spirit of God. In Matthew's version of this story, it was the "force of the wind" that gave Peter fright when he was asked to walk over the water toward Jesus. Stop for a moment and consider the symbolism of this powerful image—*the wind* was against them.

Something profound happened to Jesus in his prayer. Something courageous, something determined, something cool and calm and clear. He began to walk *on the waters*. Now he was heading defiantly back into Galilee, Herod's territory.

The chaos of this moment would terrify him no longer. The fear of dying as John had died would no longer paralyze Jesus. He would give, and give everything he had, for the sake of his hungry nation. The chaos and fear remained, but now he would walk across it with his God.

The sight of Jesus walking *on water* terrified the apostles even further. So Jesus called to them encouragingly. He used the very words that perhaps he himself had heard from his God during that long night in prayer: "'Courage! It's me! Don't be afraid.'" They took Jesus on board. He stepped into the boat with them. Immediately, *the wind* dropped. The symbolism is deeply moving.

Even more interesting is Mark's comment that the apostles found this difficult to understand precisely because "they had not seen what the miracle of the loaves meant."

To Jesus, the feeding of the crowd meant *commitment*. It meant giving one's life (or bread) for the sake of others. It meant facing the chaos and the wind and the Herods of the day with the courage and the calmness of God.

This is a story about the courage of Jesus. What a portrait of his character emerges from this supposedly simple story. In Jesus, of course, the Church sees its own capacity for courage and commitment beyond cost. If we are to understand the sort of person Jesus was or the sort of persons we all are, then we must grasp what it means "to feed the five thousand." Giving bread, or giving away everything we possess, is the best image Jesus had for describing what makes human beings happy. Generosity is the only way beyond chaos and fear.

In other words, walking on the water is a eucharistic story.

For Prayer

It is of immense importance to allow ourselves to gain a sense of the grieving Jesus. As he wept over the death of his friend Lazarus, so his grief would have been profound over the death of his close friend John.

Sit beside him on this long night and sense the silent grief and tears of loss that he is experiencing. Let any memories of your own grieving lead you into appreciating how Jesus is feeling. And the fear. The fear that what has occurred to his beloved John is but a glimpse of what might yet be in store for him should he continue to stand for the things John upheld. Jesus is shaken. Jesus needs to find the strength of his God somewhere in this overwhelming event of John's death and in his own commitment and life.

Sense how he begins to listen again to the voice of his God that night. What does he begin to "hear" in all this?

For Discussion

This is as much a story about the Church as it is about Jesus.

- The wind in Christian symbolism is the Spirit of God. What might be one headwind against which we as a Church find ourselves rowing today?
- We are aware that, as a Church, we face many issues that challenge and perhaps frighten us these days. In this story, the apostles took Jesus on board with them and the wind dropped. In practical terms today, what might it mean to take Jesus on board?
- Without indulging in criticism, we do need to reflect on our situation today. Within the Church you experience, are there signs that indicate we have yet to "take him on board" today? Speak lovingly.

10
Open Wide Your Welcome Door

So as he stepped ashore he saw a large crowd; and he took pity on them because they were like sheep without a shepherd, and he *set himself to teach them at some length.* By now it was getting very late, and his disciples came up to him and said, "This is a lonely place and it is getting very late, so send them away, and they can go to the farms and villages round about, to buy themselves something to eat." He replied, "Give them something to eat *yourselves.*" They answered, "Are we to go and spend two hundred denarii on bread *for them* to eat?" He asked, "*How many loaves have you?* Go and see." And when they had found out they said, "Five, and two fish." Then he ordered them to get all the people to sit down in groups on the green grass, and they sat down on the ground in squares of hundreds and fifties. Then *he took* the five loaves and the two fish, raised his eyes to heaven and *said the blessing;* then *he broke* the loaves and began handing them to his disciples *to distribute* among the people. He also shared out the two fish among them all. They all ate as much as they wanted. They collected *twelve basketfuls* of scraps of bread and pieces of fish. Those who had eaten the loaves numbered five thousand....

Mark 6:34–44 (emphasis added)

THIS STORY IS CENTRAL to understanding Jesus. We commonly call it the Feeding of the Five Thousand.

This is another of those stories that was used to prove Jesus was God—who else but someone "divine" could multiply the loaves and fishes. To a child's mind, this was the impressive bit! They began with just a few loaves and fish but managed to feed so many. Yet a careful reading shows that the story is not focused on the divinity of Jesus. It is focused on the sacred, disturbing, and dangerous potential of our own generosity.

This is a story in which Mark intended to show us clearly the meaning of the Eucharist. It expresses the very core of the way Jesus lived. If we had no other story about Jesus than this one, we would still see clearly what kind of person he was. This story expresses his whole way of living.

Jesus and his apostles had decided to cross Lake Galilee and go to the desert region on the far side. They were looking for "time out." In Matthew's version of the story, the reason they needed "time out" was due to shock and grief at the news of John the Baptist's death: "When Jesus received this news he withdrew by boat to a lonely place where they could be by themselves" (Matthew 14:13).

Mark used the story in a slightly different way. The apostles had just come back to Jesus after working hard in the nearby towns and villages, preaching and healing in Jesus' name. They were both weary and excited by what they had been doing. So Mark had Jesus say to them, "'Come away to some lonely place all by yourselves and rest for a while'; for there were so many coming and going that there was no time for them even to eat" (Mark 6:31).

In a sense, it matters little why they went across to the other side of Lake Galilee. What matters is that when they arrived, a large crowd had hurried there on foot and was waiting to hear more of Jesus' teaching. They were hungry for what he had to say to them.

The last thing Jesus needed at this time in his life was a noisy crowd, but their need was more urgent, so Jesus gave himself to them. His heart went out to *them*. Despite his own grieving and need for space, he made room for them in his heart. He allowed them to feed off himself yet again. In the mind of Jesus, this was the only meaning of love. When it came down to the wire, he was totally for others. Or, as he would say in more poetic form at the Last Supper,

> "My Body is given for you.
> My life is poured out for you.
> This is who I am. Do this yourselves to remember me."
> > Matthew 26:26–28, Mark 14:22–24,
> > Luke 22:19–20 (author's paraphrase)

This lakeside story is a Last Supper story. It is the Last Supper on a real day in Jesus' life. To make sure we see this, Mark was careful to use the same words in this story that he would use later when telling of the Last Supper. We will see in a moment how cleverly he arranged his eucharistic words.

The disciples were key players here. They thoughtfully noticed the lateness of the afternoon and suggested to Jesus that the crowd needed to be sent home for food and shelter.

Jesus agreed with their concern. Something had to be done. But he suggested that the apostles look after the crowd themselves! Their response was practical and, in a way, prudent. "Are you suggesting that *we* spend *our* money buying food for *them?* What business are *they* of *ours?*" (author's paraphrase).

Isn't this still the fiercest question we face today?

Jesus invited them to check their resources. The apostles looked at what they'd brought for themselves and discovered they had sufficient for their own evening meal, but nothing more. They informed Jesus of what little they had: five loaves and two fish. It was nothing in view of the crowd's size.

Jesus then did what we know as the Eucharist. He *took* what they had, and he *thanked* God for it. He then *broke* bread, telling the disciples to *give* it to the crowd. These four special words are the key words of the Last Supper. We can read them in Mark's Gospel (14:22–23).

In Mark's mind, what was happening there by the shore was

exactly what happened at the Last Supper. Mark showed us what the Eucharist means by telling us how Jesus *did* it in real life.

This is a story about the generosity and total commitment of Jesus—this is the sort of person he was. This is the Jesus whom the disciples came to know and love, who made such an impression on them that they were swept off their feet by the experience. This is the Jesus they couldn't forget. Whenever they wanted to remember what Jesus was like, they told one another *this* story. It describes his character perfectly and demonstrates in a fascinating way what Jesus meant when he spoke about "living in God."

What did the word *God* mean for Jesus? It certainly meant "to live in love." And what did Jesus think *love* meant? It clearly meant to give one's life to others with total generosity.

Jesus invited the apostles to give away everything they had. No matter how small or insufficient it seemed, he invited them to give it to the hungry crowd. He invited them to live as he lived, by being recklessly, totally generous: to take what they possessed, to thank God for having it in the first place (that's the blessing), then to use it for others—that is, to "give it away."

The truth of this frightens and astonishes us. Jesus was saying that the whole point of anyone's life is to nourish others. For Jesus, such an attitude of generosity is the one and only source of human happiness and maturity. We are here for others. He saw this as the same as being here for God. All we have and all we are is held for others. We will find our true selves—our hidden selves, or God—when we choose the way of generosity. In such dangerous generosity, one finds salvation.

This was how he lived. Desperately in need of time for himself, Jesus found himself unexpectedly confronted by a crowd. He immediately gave of himself, teaching them at some length. He was there to be consumed by them. This, in Mark's mind, is the whole meaning of the Eucharist. Catholics remind themselves of this when they call the Eucharist "a *living sacrifice* of praise."

What did *bread* mean for Jesus? What was it that fed him and kept him going in his life?

> "My food
> is to do the will of the one who sent me,
> and to complete his work."
>
> John 4:34

Bread provides a stunning insight into the person he was: "doing bread" was how he matured in life and how he came to know his God. He was nourished in the act of giving. This is why the story ends with the *twelve basketfuls of scraps.*

There were twelve apostles. Originally, they had five loaves and two fish for their own meal. Jesus challenged them to give it away—in short, to risk missing out themselves. Recklessly and generously, they rose to the challenge and did it. Yet in return, they finally collected twelve baskets of food—one for each apostle, more than they had possessed at the start.

It was in the act of giving to others that *they* were fed. Generous giving is what makes humans grow—it feeds *us.*

For Prayer

Jesus seems to have possessed the extraordinary insight that worshipping God and committing ourselves to one another in *this* world are the same thing. It was his strong conviction that the "second" commandment is *like* the "first."

So imagine you are sitting beside him in a quiet, reflective moment, perhaps enjoying together a cup of coffee. He knows you are there. He knows you well, and he uses your name when he speaks to you. This imaginative style of praying is part of the Church's long tradition of prayer and one that was used by many of the great saints.

As you sit together quietly, ask him in your own words, what does it really mean "to worship and know God"? Then listen quietly as you imagine him looking directly at you, friend with friend, and confiding to you his way of seeing things.

For Discussion

- When we celebrate the Eucharist, we are committing ourselves to something dangerous, joyful, and liberating.

    Why dangerous? Why joyful? Why liberating?

    Discuss this in terms of the story above. What is it that we go to Church to do?

- "...we offer you in thanksgiving this holy and *living* sacrifice" (emphasis added).

    These words are found right after the consecration in the third eucharistic prayer.

    What do you believe is meant by a "living" sacrifice? Who lives it? And when?

He Never Sinned

At daybreak he appeared in the Temple again; and as all the people came to him, he sat down and began to teach them.

The scribes and Pharisees brought a woman along who had been caught committing adultery; and *making her stand there in the middle* they said to Jesus, "Master, this woman was caught in the very act of committing adultery, and in the Law Moses has ordered us to stone women of this kind. *What have you got to say?*" They asked him this as a test, *looking for an accusation to use against him.* But Jesus bent down and started writing on the ground with his finger. As they persisted with their question, he straightened up and said, "Let the one among you who is guiltless be the first to throw a stone at her." Then he bent down and continued writing on the ground. When they heard this they went away one by one, *beginning with the eldest,* until the last one had gone and Jesus was left alone with the woman, *who remained in the middle.* Jesus again straightened up and said, "*Woman, where are they? Has no one condemned you?*" "No one, sir," *she replied.* "Neither do I condemn you," said Jesus. "Go away, and from this moment *sin no more.*"

John 8:1–11 (emphasis added)

JESUS NEVER SINNED. He was like us in all things, but he never sinned. He was tempted in every way that we are, but he always said, "Yes" to the Spirit of God that was deep inside himself. When pushed to the limit, he always chose to love more deeply—to love even these hardheaded scribes and Pharisees.

As mentioned earlier, one important meaning of the Jewish word for *sin* is "to miss the target" (like an arrow). Jesus never sinned.

He never allowed himself to be distracted (as we often are) from seeing the *real* issue in question. It was not easy for him to do this—indeed, he would have been severely tempted by the pig-headedness of the accusers in this story. But there was more at stake than simply their stupidity and cunning. His first priority was the terrified woman.

She was made to stand there "in the middle," in full view of everybody, deeply shamed and frightened. Let's not forget that she fully expected to be executed; she was a few moments from death. It is difficult for us to imagine how distraught and frightened she was.

Jesus knew it. He knew something of what she was going through. Like hers, his own life was already in deep water. He felt for her with a compassion that came from shared experience, fear, and uncertainty.

The scribes and Pharisees had no sense of this pain at all. They were intent on scoring points for their own position. They judged people. They were abusing this woman by using her as a pawn to entrap Jesus. They had no sense of her God-given dignity. For them she was simply a means to an end.

In this they had lost all sense of their own dignity as well. They seemed incapable of taking personal authority for their own stance in life. They justified their attitude by appealing to Moses. What Moses had decreed so long ago, and in different times, they would unthinkingly follow at this time. They saw no need for personal decision making on the issue—what Moses once said dictated the path. Foolishly, they called this "tradition."

For Jesus, there was a deeper tradition: the sacredness of all persons. If all women and men were made in the very likeness of his God, then they had rights to be so respected and treated. The God he knew was a God of *life,* not of death. For Jesus, there was more to the mystery of this God he loved than what could be contained in human law and custom, no matter how "sacred" some might call such "traditions."

Jesus could not recognize these "religious" people as being true to the tradition. They had turned it into something shallow, something demeaning, something to be used against others. They had lost the heart of it all. Overcome with sadness at the position they espoused, he was quite unable to speak with them.

He bought time by writing on the ground. He chose not to be engaged with them on their terms. He used silence to put pressure back onto them. Unthinkingly, they merely persisted with their opening challenge. Obviously, they could not see the real issues at stake.

Silence didn't work, so Jesus applied more pressure, this time using a return question that changed the whole dynamic of the confrontation. He dared any one of them to publicly declare himself free of sinful experience. In responding with such a question, he left them with their dignity intact. They were free to declare themselves—the choice was theirs. He didn't corner them by pronouncement; he appealed to them by question. It was not a choice they had given to the woman.

The older among them were the wisest. Life had taught them the realities of our shared sinful condition. It was not so much that Jesus had caught them, but his question triggered memories of how *life* catches all of us in struggle, in sin, and in hypocrisy of one kind or another. And to a degree, they were finally courageous enough to admit it.

And the woman?

For one thing, the way Jesus acted immediately took the heat off her. He wasn't distracted by her apparent sin from sensing the *real* issue at stake. He was fighting for her. He took her side and in public. Alone among the crowd she found this one man who refused to be her enemy. He sensed more in her than what she had done. Her sinfulness didn't distract him from a deeper, more life-giving truth about her. Jesus didn't sin. He didn't miss the point of it all. She was made in God's image, and Jesus treated her as such. Although she was stripped of her dignity and self-esteem, he returned it to her by his silent, steely refusal to play the judgmental games of others. She meant more in his eyes than that. He would pass no judgment that would wound her further. Her life was struggle enough without such added burden. He loved something in her that others had never seen.

So she remained standing there. No longer held there by force, she now chose to stay in front of this unusual man. She had sensed something in his eye and attitude that she had never before experienced from others. She felt secure enough to recover her personal authority—she *decided* to stay. In her frighteningly public exposure, he sheltered her. In his sheltering, she grew.

More than this, Jesus now addressed her directly, person to person. The interaction was so normal that there's a danger we can miss the extraordinariness of what was happening.

He covered for her; he fought for her; he valued her person.

Recovering from her distress, she sensed the value she held in his eyes; she took her life in hand and chose to stay.

So they conversed, woman and man, eye to eye, heart to heart. They did so in public view. Jesus' questions, "Woman, where are they? Has no one condemned you?" were almost playful in their phrasing. One can only hope some day to know what it must have meant for Jesus to see someone like this woman reaching for her freedom and her life again. What profound pleasure it must have given him! What memories he would carry for life of God's power at work in her. Meeting a woman of such character, one capable of such a courageous and public response, would have made everything in his life worthwhile.

It is no wonder Jesus could not condemn her. He was being realistic about the unfortunate ways she had tried to love in her life (her sin), but he was being just as realistic about her potential to love more responsibly. He urged her to discontinue her current ways and to release a larger love in her life.

Given the courage and character she had already shown, he had every reason to believe she would take the opportunity he was offering. There was more to loving than she had realized. Given the chance, she began to believe in her own capacity to love and to live for others. Her loving would be more life-giving than ever—she had seen Jesus doing exactly this for her. She loved him for the way he had "saved" her and stood beside her. She could do the same. She had seen her better self mirrored in his courage and compassion.

For Prayer

Imagine it is early evening on that same day. Jesus has found some solitude out on the hills to reflect upon what has occurred during the day.

You watch him sitting, or standing quietly, allowing the memories of the morning to flood back into his mind and heart. Sense within yourself how pleasant for Jesus is the memory of that woman. He warms to her courage and strength.

He remembers how surprised he was to look up and realize she was still standing there, unforced, in front of him. What feelings does this memory evoke in Jesus? What does the memory of this woman do for his sense of commitment to justice and to the liberation of his beloved people?

As you sense his feelings, enjoy them as your own. Let them find a home in your own heart and mind.

For Discussion

- From the evidence of this story, what does it mean to forgive sin?
- In scriptural language, the word *sin* means "to miss the point." We all too easily miss the point of our lives, or

miss the life-giving point in some delicate or important relationship. This affects each time the potential within ourselves to grow into the maturity of God's freedom and responsibility.

What difference does such a meaning bring to your understanding of sin?

- The Church is called to be the great sign of forgiveness in today's harsh and demeaning world. This is why we call the Church "a sacrament of forgiveness." It is our privilege to be this sign of hope—to be for the world and its peoples what Jesus was for this woman.

Is there anything in this story of the adulterous woman that might alert us to how God is challenging us to grow as a forgiving Church today?

12
To Have a Mind Like Jesus'

Now there was a woman who had suffered from a haemorrhage for twelve years; after long and painful treatment under various doctors, *she had spent all she had* without being any the better for it; in fact, *she was getting worse.* She had heard about Jesus, and she came up through the crowd and touched his cloak from behind, thinking, "*If I can just touch his clothes,* I shall be saved." And at once the source of the bleeding dried up, and *she felt in herself that she was cured* of her complaint.

And at once aware of the power that had gone out from him, Jesus turned round in the crowd and said, "*Who touched my clothes?*" His disciples said to him, "You see how the crowd is pressing round you; how can you ask, '*Who touched me?*'" But he continued to look all round to see who had done it. *Then the woman came forward,* frightened and trembling because *she knew what had happened to her,* and she fell at his feet and *told him the whole truth.* "My daughter," he said, "*your faith* has restored you to health; go in peace and be free of your complaint."

Mark 5:25–34 (emphasis added)

THIS EXTRAORDINARY STORY gives us a vivid insight into the consciousness of Jesus and in an awesome way outlines the humility of the man.

Humility is not a "popular" term. Interestingly, it is based on the Latin *humus,* meaning "of the soil" or "of the earth."

In today's world of competitiveness, image-making, self-esteem, and promotional advertising, humility is not highly valued. Our style of society has lost its taste for humility and noncompetitiveness. It's no wonder that as we read the stories of the gospel, our ears and hearts are no longer attuned to this lovable human quality in Jesus.

In my younger years as a Catholic, in such stories as this, we looked for the "Lord" or for the "Divine Master" (the "God"), failing to perceive the more delicate—and lovable—outlines of this humble man's mind and heart. This was the mind-set of the Church of that era. We were captured by the "divine nature" of the Church to which we belonged. In some ways, during the pre–Vatican II years, our Catholic focus was on the next world, the world of the supernatural. Accordingly, the only Jesus we were capable of seeing in the gospels reflected this focus of our lives: he was all-knowing and divinely gifted. Jesus was from—and of—another world.

Such an exalted Jesus could be worshiped and adored—even followed. But it was difficult to fall in love with someone so *un*like our human selves. To stress (as the gospels do) his humanity is not to deny the divine reality of Jesus. But the gospels do suggest that the deepest core of all humanness is ultimately where the divine is to be found. In Jesus, God is seen as *humus,* of the soil and earth of which we are all made. How profoundly *humus* he was is a realization that will bring us into awesome reverence and contemplation.

This woman was seriously ill and desperately poor. She had come to the end of her tether after twelve years of illness, embarrassment, and mistreatment. But now she had "heard" of Jesus. Stripped of everything except her hope, her courage, and her faith, she determined to touch just his garment in one final admission of her profound need for God's help.

Clearly, a physical miracle occurred here. The source of her bleeding was healed. She knew instantly that she was cured. Something most unusual and real had happened. Here an intervention of God had taken place. She knew it in her bones. She was in tune with her body and her spirit—she knew what had happened "from the inside."

And so did Jesus. He was immediately aware that power "had gone out from him." Something had leaped between his spirit and the kindred spirit of someone in that crowd. There was someone nearby who had drawn Spirit from him, and Jesus was sensitive to that layer of reality. Surrounded by dozens of people, jostled and involved with them, he still listened at all levels of his being. He had learned to be attentive to what was occurring deeper than consciousness. Even as part of a noisy crowd, Jesus maintained his inner poise. He was at heart a listener, and his inner ear registered the touch of someone's *faith*, the nearness of someone's courage and desperation.

This inner sense was the fruit of his prayer. His frequent and long hours of contemplation awoke in Jesus this "inner sense" of beauty, truth, and need. It is a sense we all possess in seed. It is a capacity that our civilization largely has lost, but which is still enjoyed by many Easterners and by people of cultures that remain in touch with nature. In Jesus it was cultivated, nurtured, and matured. He *felt* through his bones the passage of power. Something healing had occurred as the Spirit leaped from him to her.

Perhaps our scientific approach to life distrusts such things. It's as if today we believe that for every healing there is a medical explanation. What is challenged in us is our pride. We find it difficult to admit that something might simply be "beyond us."

This flies in the face of wider human experience in cultures different from ours. Aboriginal people experience dimensions of life that we do not understand. Perhaps our ultimate and humbling admission must be that we simply do not know it all. The sacred is real. This woman knew it: she touched, and she was cured.

Jesus, of course, would protest that the sacred she touched was within herself. Driven by desperation, she reached down into her

deepest levels of faith, trust, conviction, and personal humility—
and she released the healing powers of God who lay within them
both. Jesus didn't doubt for a moment whose faith had triggered
the cure: "'...*your* faith has restored you to health; go in peace and
be free of your complaint'" (emphasis added).

Notice how attuned Jesus was to the sacred within the woman.
He named *her* faith as something *he* admired. There were no pre-
tensions about him. He took nothing to himself in this encounter
but attributed it directly to the courage and faith of the woman
who considered herself a nobody. When the crowd was challenged,
she didn't need to come forward and be identified. She was already
sure of her cure. But she made a choice, and taking her courage in
her hands, she went public, falling at his feet in gratitude and telling him "the whole truth."

And it was Jesus who was amazed at the quality of her faith.

His habitual attitude seems to have been to notice the heroic in
others. It happens constantly in stories like this. It's as if he took
upon himself the delightful task of noticing and then affirming in
public the goodness and heroism he saw in the little people around
him, in those people whom most had already dismissed as unwor-
thy of consideration. This was his habit of mind, his normal outlook on life—to find, to name, and to build the sacred within others. Jesus would be the earth in which *they* grew, and in contact
with him they would recognize *their own maturity and potential.*
He would simply be the occasion for them to recognize themselves.
He saw himself as being thereby at the service of their sacredness.
He washed their feet. They fed on him.

The way Jesus saw himself is profoundly different from any suggestion that he knew he was God. He carried no airs. He did not
see himself as superior. His humility was so profound that it is
beyond our experience and conception—a humility so basic that
we find it difficult to appreciate because we never dwell in humility long enough to know it. We do not value—or recognize—how

sacred the *humus* in one's life can be. We turn our fascinations upon those who are powerful and significant in life.

Jesus, on the contrary, recognized this humble, uncomplicated woman. He was on eye-level with her. He could "see" her with clarity. She was of the dust of which he was made. Her sense of desperation was one he knew well himself. He "recognized" her faith and her courage. It was bone of his bone and flesh of his flesh. This woman and Jesus stood on common soil. The quality of her heroism, the greatness of her apparently small life, was instantly perceived by Jesus—this was his mind. The greatness of the man lay in the depth of his own humility.

This quality was what endeared Jesus to those who knew him well and who followed him closely. They watched him, they fell in love with what they saw, and they were determined to remember him forever. This was why, years later, Paul would write these astonishing words to the Church at Philippi:

> ...out of humility of mind everyone should give preference to others, everyone pursuing not selfish interests but those of others. *Make your own the mind of Christ Jesus....*
>
> Philippians 2:3–5 (emphasis added)

For Prayer

Imagine you are watching Jesus as he is lost in his own private prayer. Observe him closely. Imagine what is going through his mind as the memories of this woman come back to him. How clearly he recalls the experience of "something going out of himself." As he prays, he is in that moment of awareness again, and something leaps from deep inside himself. There is someone nearby to whom his deepest spirit has *involuntarily responded*. Someone in this crowd has reached him at his deepest level. What a mystery it is when Spirit calls to Spirit. Allow Jesus to ponder the mystery of this truth that God lives in the depths of all of us.

Take time to enjoy this prayer.

Or...

In his mind's eye he sees the woman. He loves her for her faith. He is in utter admiration of her courage and touched by her desperation. Sense the feelings in him as he contemplates in silence the woman he met that day. What are his feelings for her?

Take time to enjoy this prayer.

For Discussion

- There must be no competition among you, no conceit; but everybody is to be self-effacing. Always consider the other person to be better than yourself so that nobody thinks of their own interests first, but everybody thinks of other people's interests instead. In short, in your minds you must be the same as Christ Jesus (author's paraphrase of Philippians 2:2–5).

  Who, being in the form of God,
  did not count equality with God
  something to be grasped.

  But he emptied himself,
  taking the form of a slave,
  becoming as human beings are;

  and being *in every way like a human being*,
  he was humbler yet,
  even to accepting death, death on a cross.
  Philippians 2:6–8 (emphasis added)

Saint Paul was overwhelmed by the mind of Jesus that he here described. Read it carefully together and discuss any aspect of Paul's writing that appeals to you.

What phrase is most startling to you?

Why might it be so?

13
Until Christ and Earth Are One

They reached the territory of the Gerasenes on *the other side* of the lake, and when he disembarked, a man with an unclean spirit at once came out from the tombs towards him. The man *lived in the tombs* and no one could secure him any more, even with a chain…no one had *the strength to control him.* All night and all day, among the tombs and in the mountains, he would *howl and gash himself with stones.* Catching sight of Jesus from a distance, he ran up and fell at his feet and shouted at the top of his voice, "What do you want with me, Jesus, son of the Most High God? In God's name do not torture me!" For Jesus had been saying to him, "Come out of the man, unclean spirit." Then he asked, *"What is your name?"* He answered, "My name is Legion, for there are many of us." And he begged him earnestly not to send them out of the district. Now on the mountainside there was a great herd of *pigs feeding,* and the unclean spirits begged him, "Send us to the pigs, let us go into them." So he gave them leave. With that, the unclean spirits came out and went into the pigs, and the herd of about two thousand pigs charged down the cliff *into the lake,* and there they were drowned. The men looking after them ran off and told their story in the city and in the country round about; and the people came to see what had really happened. They came to Jesus and saw the demoniac sitting there—the man who had had the legion in him—*properly dressed* and *in his full senses,* and *they were afraid.* And those who had witnessed it reported what had happened to the demoniac and what had become of the pigs. *Then they began to implore Jesus to leave their neighbourhood.* As he was getting into the boat, the man who had been possessed begged to be allowed to stay with him. Jesus would not let him but said to him, *"Go home to your people and tell them* all that the Lord in his mercy has done for you." So the man went off and proceeded to proclaim in the Decapolis all that Jesus had done for him. And everyone was amazed.

Mark 5:1–20 (emphasis added)

THIS EVENT MAY HAVE happened on one real day in the life of Jesus. Whether or not it happened in real life makes no difference to the truth and value of *its meaning for us*. Here is expressed in poetic story form the meaning of Jesus' life and its impact on the people around him. Here is expressed powerfully the sort of person his disciples knew him to be.

Jesus is here portrayed as the one who "took on" the spirit of evil in our world. This is why he came. This is what all human life is about. This is a story about the difference *our* lives can make. This is why it is called a myth. It carries crucial meaning for *us,* a meaning that, should we fail to catch it properly, will leave our lives the poorer.

Jesus crossed to "the other side." Had he chosen to stay on his own side of the lake, the encounter described here would not have happened. He could have stayed in his own familiar territory. But he was baptized, publicly committed to God's interests. So, baptized, he crossed to the other side on mission.

On "the other side," he was confronted by someone who inhabited the tombs, the places of the dead. The life of this sad person was violence itself. He was treated with violence; his own language was violence. He had become nobody's responsibility, and completely out of control, he belonged among the dead. Poignantly, he himself was the major victim of his own harsh condition: "All night and all day, among the tombs and in the mountains, he would howl and gash himself with stones." Society had given up on him. It was impossible to do anything for him—things had gone too far. This sad and broken creature had become a caricature of that "image and likeness of God" in which he was first made.

What he did "image" was the society into which Jesus had been born. Possessed by a spirit of torment, the nation itself was living among the tombs of its own hopes and dreams, a sad shadow of the lovely entity it could have been. This growing kingdom of evil was a cause of deep sadness in Jesus, for it was his own people who were most violated in this experience. Yet unlike others, Jesus believed that things were not beyond challenge and hope. He would confront with his life this spirit that possessed his people. He loved them far too much to leave them languishing among the tombs of their life and times. This story expresses the myth that drove Jesus in his life.

The evil spirit tried to name Jesus. In Jewish culture, to name something (or someone) was to have power. If I named it, then I owned it. Fathers "named" their children. Adam and Eve (in the Garden of Eden story) were invited by God "to name" the animals. Jesus called his apostles and gave them special "names." And here, the spirit of evil was trying to own Jesus by naming him first.

Jesus did not respond to the attempt to "name" him. He would not allow the spirit of evil any power over him. Instead, Jesus took the offensive and demanded the name of the spirit! The calm strength and personal authority of Jesus could not be broken by the evil around him. He took on the spirits head-on. He was unafraid.

It was the spirits who were cowering now. They had met their match in Jesus. They submitted to his questioning and gave way before his strength and character. They pleaded and begged even to be "allowed" to inhabit pigs. In Jewish culture, this was the ultimate indignity: pigs were the lowest of the low. Jesus dismissed them for what they were and "let them go" to the pigs. The herd rushed into the depths of the lake—almost as if the evil spirits were rushing home to where all hell and chaos belonged, beneath the seething waters.

Jesus and the spirits had clashed. But let the raciness of the story not distract us from the love Jesus held for this broken, violated man—symbol of his people.

The moment Jesus landed on the shore he was aware of the man's predicament. Unlike others, Jesus stood his ground as the demoniac ran toward him. Jesus' heart was broken by the man's pitiable situation, and he would not leave him alone to suffer as he had suffered so far. Sensing the potential for life, Jesus chose not to believe that death and violence had the final word. He would fight for the one possessed, whom Jesus saw as "bone of his bone and flesh of his flesh."

The confrontation was severe, the outcome serene. By the time the people had gathered, this once-demonic man was "sitting there" at the feet of Jesus, "clothed and in his full senses." Just taking time to contemplate this lovely image in our hearts is to contemplate the mystery of who was Jesus.

It was the people, of course, who were now afraid. Their world had been turned on its ear. Something beyond all human expectation was happening among them. They were implicated. Where could this all end? What did this man's truth and courage mean for their own shallow lives? Their foolishly structured world held no room for the unpredictable ways of God. Things were changing too rapidly for them. It was easier and clearer when a demoniac was a demoniac and knew his place—in the tombs. They were afraid of the proximity of goodness and courage, for it meant change and growth in themselves. They begged Jesus to leave them alone. They begged him to go.

Yet one of them had returned to his "full senses." One of them had experienced the liberation of God's proximity. One of them was capable of believing in his own capacity to do as Jesus did and to take up his life with authority as he had seen Jesus do. One of them had been "baptized": blown into a new world by this encounter with goodness.

Jesus and his disciples left, and the man once possessed remained there but now *with a mission*. In his customary way, Jesus had immediately sensed his potential. Now baptized by his encounter with Jesus, the man would embody it fully.

Is there any wonder the Church would come to call such an experience "salvation"? And what an insight lies here for us about the meaning of baptism? Confronted by the person of Jesus, this man's previous existence was blown away completely, and in its place was a burning mission to proclaim that same Jesus everywhere.

"'Go home to your people and tell them all that the Lord in his mercy has done for you.' So the man went off and proceeded to proclaim...all that Jesus had done for him."

For Prayer

In your mind's eye, see Jesus arriving on the shore, stepping out of the boat, already alerted to the presence in the nearby hills of this wailing, broken creature. The apostles hold back in fear, but Jesus moves up the shoreline, looking for the desperate demoniac. Watch Jesus, as if you are there right beside him, and hear him praying quietly and earnestly for his deliverance. Let grow within yourself that sense of quiet determination that is in Jesus, that fire for liberation that fills him in that moment.

Or...

Let yourself be one of the apostles as you sit somewhere nearby and you are gazing quietly at the picture of Jesus standing there, waiting for the townspeople to come up, with the once-possessed man now sitting calmly and alert at Jesus' feet. Watch the interaction between them. The apostles have given him some of their clothing. Contemplate them—watch Jesus and the man together. Let the beauty of the image touch your heart and spirit.

For Discussion

- What occurred in the life of Jesus is occurring in society today.

   What is your experience? Are there people "living among the tombs" today?

   Are there those who gash themselves with stones?

Are there those whom society has given up on? Those whom "no one has the strength to control"?

- Jesus "crossed to the other side." Discuss the implications of this for the Church, for your parish, or for your school. What might it mean for us to "cross to the other side"?

- A myth gives us energy for life. What effect do you notice this story has in yourself?

- A myth will work its effect in us only if our contact with it is constant and regular. How can your group (parish, staff) improve its contact with these gospel stories?

14
Beyond the Fears That Close Me In

After this, Jesus travelled round Galilee; *he could not travel round Judaea,* because the Jews were seeking *to kill him.*

John 7:1 (emphasis added)

From that day onwards *they were determined to kill him.* So Jesus no longer went about openly among the Jews, but *left the district* for a town called Ephraim, in the country bordering on the desert, and stayed there with his disciples.

John 11:53–54 (emphasis added)

"I have come to bring *fire to the earth,* and how I wish it were blazing already! There is a *baptism* I must still receive, and *what constraint I am under* until it is completed!"

Luke 12:49–50 (emphasis added)

Now...as the time drew near...*he resolutely turned his face towards Jerusalem.*

Luke 9:51 (emphasis added)

IT IS DIFFICULT to know exactly the daily and monthly pattern of Jesus' public life. Commentators try to harmonize the four gospel stories to discover the underlying chronology, but it is not possible. The gospels are not newspapers. They never tried to tell his life's story in such detail. They are four different collections of sayings and stories that are more or less similar, about one real person's life. They are memories of *the sort of person he was*—not detailed accounts of his everyday activities. As memories of his character, they are true and accurate. They depict his struggle and triumph. The greatness of Jesus burned itself into the hearts and minds of his followers, and they never wanted to forget this person they knew.

Each writer of the gospel gave us a different impression of his greatness. Different aspects of his character became precious to different communities of Christians. It was in these different communities that the gospels were written; they reflected the special memories each community held of him. Yet in a lovely way, they all managed to say the same basic truth about the person he was. The whole collection of their memories—*four* gospels—gives us a consistent picture of his character, his spirit, his faith, and his journey through the turmoil of his public life. In all the gospels, his life ended in *Jerusalem.*

Jesus was a Jew, and the heartland of his life was Jerusalem. It was the sacred city; it embodied the whole tradition. It represented the heart and soul of Jewish faith and pride. The city stood for their faith; it symbolized their identity as a nation of God. It was the seat of power. In short, Jerusalem was Judaism.

Jesus grew up in Galilee, and it was in that northern region that most of his public life was spent. The lake of Galilee somehow captured the heart of his ministry and work. Many of his followers came from there. The Galilee months were the springtime of their lives with him.

He did experience opposition and criticism in Galilee, but nothing like the opposition and threat that would come from Jerusalem—the nation's center. His work and teaching among the poor and the dispossessed threatened to unravel the whole social fabric of the nation. The way he related to people, and the way he imagined people of all classes could relate to one another, disturbed those layers of society that benefited from the established order of things. For Jesus, all of God's people, sinners and saints, were welcome "at the meal" of God's kingdom. The gospels described him constantly "at table" with the poor, the outcast, the sinners—as well as with Pharisees and the rich. Meals seem to summarize his vision of what we long for in our deepest hearts. In his eating with sinners, Jesus expressed in a sign-language that all can grasp what the justice of his God truly means. The world can be like this: common-table is our hope. We are capable of the openness, love, and acceptance that shared-table demands. In a world savagely divided by class, race, religion, gender, and national competitiveness, a simple shared table becomes the icon of our hope.

In this sense, Jesus was a revolutionary. This genial outlaw possessed a vision of what God's kingdom *could* be, and it seriously threatened the power and position of those who held authority in the current kingdom. When finally the powerful accused him of sedition and revolution, let's realize how truthfully they meant such words. His life profoundly disturbed Jewish society. He challenged the order of things. He spoke of change. He was too free. The things he did dared others to conversion of life. His words stirred new imaginings and dangerous freedoms. No one knew where they stood any more. He opposed legitimate authority.

They called him the devil incarnate. Some tried to dismiss him as a passing phenomenon, a hothead out of Galilee, a nobody. Others could not tolerate the blasphemy they perceived his life to be and, for the honor of the God in which they believed, were prepared to kill him: "'It is better for one man to die for the people'" (John 18:14).

And so Jesus, fearing for his life, began to avoid Jerusalem. He had sufficient Pharisee friends to know the pressure that was building against him. Frightened by the prospect of what had occurred to John the Baptist, Jesus backed off to avoid the confrontation. Afraid for his life, confused and uncertain about what to do in the face of such hostility, he gained time by "leaving town."

> After this, Jesus travelled round Galilee; *he could not travel round Judaea,* because the Jews were seeking *to kill him.*
>
> John 7:1 (emphasis added)

When we overly emphasize the divinity of Jesus, this human reaction to threats on his life is confusing. We see such a "divine" Jesus as somehow still in control of his life, choosing to avoid the dangerous confrontation because he knew in some mystical way that it was "not yet his time."

But how much more lovable and admirable is the real Jesus of the gospels, the one who was afraid? More like us than we dare to admit, he needed space to come to terms with what was happening. This was "the wilderness" into which the Spirit had "driven him." And he found it a severe temptation.

Jesus had to make decisions about his life just as we do. He possessed no map, no program that made it all plain to him. Coming to clarity about what was to be the next step in his life was a lengthy and challenging process. It was his life that was on the line, and his integrity. The inner turmoil of such a decision cannot be imagined by those of us who have never found ourselves so faced. For Jesus, Jerusalem was coming to represent, potentially, the most momentous decision of his life. It all turned on Jerusalem. This was the place of commitment and danger. For how much longer in his life could he afford to avoid the pain of facing this truth?

In a sense, Jesus was trapped by his own faith. His public baptismal commitment already had him cornered. His words about love, about throwing one's life away for others, about courage and justice and God, had webbed him in. He could live with himself no longer if he could not face Jerusalem—he could not stay true and keep running. Jerusalem represented that "baptism of fire" he could no longer avoid:

"There is a *baptism* I must still receive, and *what constraint I am under* until it is completed!"

Luke 12:50 (emphasis added)

There was no way out. The only way forward was to love his people even more deeply and to entrust his poor life to the Father even more consciously. For he was coming to realize that his life would become a sham if he could not step with courage "beyond the fears that closed him in." He could not keep avoiding the issue and still remain true to himself.

It was either fear or love—one could not live in both. Within the clarity of these alternatives, the flint of his character emerged. Jesus set himself resolutely toward that final confrontation. He determined to face them in Jerusalem; there was simply no other way to be true to his deepest self. The time had come....

Now...as the time drew near...*he resolutely turned his face towards Jerusalem.*

Luke 9:51 (emphasis added)

If we miss the sacredness of such decision making, what a tragedy that would be. Being decisive is the fabric of all human life. Decisions around integrity confront us constantly in daily life. As they were for him, so they are for us, sacramental moments—sacred moments when choices to love more deeply confront us, and our lives can break through into new levels of commitment and fulfillment. In marriages, families, relationships, and work, pain-filled decisions to face the implications of commitments we have made are a normal part of human maturity—it is how we grow into who we can be. Decisions confront us with our *potential to love*; they fashion us either into or away from the truth of our being.

Unlike us, Jesus never sinned. His decision to finally face the truth (symbolized by Jerusalem) uncovered that "hidden self" that grows strong only through ever deeper loving.

Jesus was haunted by his own beliefs: if "our virtue goes no deeper than that of the scribes and Pharisees, then we will never know the kingdom of heaven" (Matthew 5:20; author's paraphrase). Jerusalem challenged *his* virtue.

Unless our compassion can flow as deeply as the compassion of the Father, then we will never know true freedom of spirit (Luke 6:36). Jerusalem challenged *his* compassion.

It was ultimately his compassion that turned Jesus toward Jerusalem: compassion for the poor, the voiceless, the little people of his day. It was finally his loyalty to them that drove him "beyond the fears that closed him in."

For Prayer

There is something buried deep within us that already knows how Jesus prayed. When we contemplate him at prayer, something inside us "knows" by intuition what is occurring within him.

Imagine you are somewhere nearby as Jesus is lost in prayer. This is the prayer time in which he finally resolves to go to Jerusalem, no matter what the cost. Something breaks inside him, and he is no longer bound by his fear. He becomes decisive and calm. He will go to Jerusalem. The Father is with him in a new way.

Quietly, in your heart's eye, watch this change work its way into Jesus. Sense in your heart what occurs in his. Be real about the doubts and fears he experiences. Begin by being real about how desperately he needs to pray, needs to find a deeper freedom and clarity about his life. Begin by becoming real about the uneasiness he feels in continuing to avoid Jerusalem.

For Discussion

- The gospels portray a Jesus who struggled with decisions as we do. Clarity concerning what steps to take in his life came to him gradually. What dignity does this give to us in our own life's journey?

Is there some way of effectively teaching our children about a Jesus as real as this?

- The Church sees itself as always being in need of deeper conversion to the gospels. The Latin phrase used for this is *Ecclesia semper reformanda* ("the Church always needing conversion"). Discuss one experience of being Church today in which you see we are beginning to move into a deeper gospel conversion.

- The Church is like Jesus as it journeys through its life and history. In a loving way, discuss what might be one Jerusalem in our life as Church today which we would prefer not to approach for fear of what it might cost us.

How will it become possible for us to grow in the courage to face such a Jerusalem together? What steps do you believe we must first have in place if similar courage and love are to emerge among us?

15
Against the Tide

As he drew near and came in sight of the city *he shed tears* over it and said, "If you too had only recognised on this day the way to peace! But in fact it is hidden from your eyes!"

Luke 19:41–42 (emphasis added)

"Jerusalem, Jerusalem, you that kill the prophets and stone those who are sent to you! How often have I *longed to gather your children together,* as a hen gathers her brood under her wings, and you refused!"

Luke 13:34 (emphasis added)

In 1907 CARL JUNG commented that Western societies had lost their capacity to think symbolically. As a result, he added, he would expect the sacramental systems of Western churches to soon fall into disarray. He certainly had insight. We have seen that the task the Church has set itself in this latter half of the twentieth century is precisely to reform its sacramental, symbolic rituals.

If we can begin to think *symbolically* of the gospels again (which is the way they were written in the first place), we would gather enormous insight into our lives with God.

Jerusalem was a symbol in the gospels. It was, of course, very real as a city. But it stood for more in the life of Jesus than being simply a city. This is what we mean when we say something is a symbol—it "stands for more" than might at first appear.

Jesus was a Jew. For him, Jerusalem somehow captured what it meant to be Jewish. This beautiful city, high on the mountains of Judaea, was a sight for all nations to see. This was no ordinary city—this was the city of God. It stood for God's justice and peace. In it could be found the very Temple of God. It would endure forever as a sign of how faithful God would be to the Jewish people. In the marriage between God and the Jewish people, Jerusalem was like the precious ring on the bride's finger. The city was a sign of God's presence and would always be so.

Jerusalem represented the dream of Jesus. No Jew could have a national dream that didn't include Jerusalem. The early Church saw themselves the same way—the "new" Jerusalem, coming down from heaven as beautiful as a bride prepared for her husband:

> "Look, here God lives among human beings. He will make *his home among them; they will be his people,* and he will be their God, *God-with-them. He will wipe* away all *tears from their eyes;* there will be no more death, and no more mourning or sadness or pain. The world of the past has gone."
>
> Revelation 21:3–4

The public life of Jesus could be summarized by such a dream for his people. This was how he began his preaching in the synagogue at Nazareth, and it had been the same fierce message of John the Baptist whom he loved so dearly:

> "…he has anointed me
> to bring the good news to the afflicted.
> He has sent me to proclaim liberty to captives,
> sight to the blind,
> to let the oppressed go free,
> *to proclaim a year of favour from the Lord."*
>
> Luke 4:18–19

What was God's "year of favour"? It was simple and very basic. Every seventh year all debts were to be canceled. This ideal, sometimes written into Jewish legislation, was a net to catch the very poor and to prevent their being bound into poverty and debt all their lives. It was a way of expressing in law the loving justice of God. Intended to preserve the dignity of even the poorest in matters economic, sadly it was neglected more than honored. But as an ideal it captured the enticing image of God's "new time." It was a symbol for the passionate preaching of both Jesus and his cousin John.

Like John, Jesus hoped for a spiritual awakening in the nation that would usher in this "new time" of God. Both of them challenged the nation to live God's justice in a new way. It was the national mentality that their preaching threatened, a mentality that oppressed the little people, the battlers of Israel; a mentality that created insiders and outsiders, the saved and the damned. In the mind of Jesus, Israel could regain its "heart of flesh" and leave aside forever the "heart of stone" that it was presently living. Repent! Be converted! Change your heart! Become once more a nation noted for its forgiveness, compassion, and loving justice, a nation in which laws and customs served the needs of people, and not vice versa. The capacity was there. It lies deep in every human heart. Jesus set himself to uncover that capacity and to show by his own manner of living just how easily—and happily—such Jewish dreams were realizable. His life would show that a "new time" was upon them by proclaiming that a never-ending "year of favour" was within their reach. All it needed was a revolution in attitudes to God and to one another—mere openness of heart.

The dreams of Jesus were intensely social. For him, attitudes to others mapped our attitudes to God. The second commandment "to love others" was *like* the first commandment "to love God." There was no distinction between them for Jesus. His unusually disturbing insight was that God is as near as our neighbor and as visible as the social realities that surround us. This is the sort of person he was, and a new-hearted nation of justice represented the hopes he held. Jerusalem embodied it all—his hopes, his dreams, his longings and loves and vision.

Yet it all failed. His dream died. His vision was not shared. His longings were matched by the merest few, and his hopes lay scattered. Seemingly, it was all over. One can barely imagine the feelings in his heart as finally he neared the city of Jerusalem and caught sight of it—the city!

> As he drew near and came in sight of the city *he shed tears* over it and said, "If you too had only recognised on this day the way to peace! But in fact it is hidden from your eyes!"
>
> Luke 19:41–42 (emphasis added)

There is a failure in the work of Jesus that we find hard to accept. He had given so much, risked everything he had, and his life was rushing to finality—and still Jerusalem faced him across the valley, unrepentant, arrogant, and menacing. This was to be his final confrontation with hope.

Everything he longed for was gone. Something grand and beautiful was dying within himself. So Jesus wept. Grieving, he wept.

The stupidity of it all; the silliness and blindness of it all; the self-destructiveness of it all; the waste. Facing the city, he was one small man. He stood alone against the tide of human apathy and disinterest. It broke his heart. Was this the end of the road? Did it all come down to this? What really had his life achieved? The bitterness of his disappointment could be measured only by his tears and by any who know this same experience. Jerusalem, across the valley, was challenging the life out of him.

Jesus had to let go of his dream. It was as if his tears washed away something profound from his own heart and mind, as if he needed to baptize with tears *his* plans for God's people.

And once he had shed himself of his own hopes and dreams,

then and then only was he able to stand with something like a new freedom before this city. Then and then only was he able to walk calmly—and in faith—into the only Jerusalem that awaited him. Not the Jerusalem of his dreams, but the Jerusalem of God's hidden presence. This was what Jesus now had to trust: that his Father was *there*—in *this* Jerusalem. It was as if his tears had to purify the eyes of his heart into "*Thy* kingdom come," not mine.

For Prayer

A passage in the gospels will come alive for us only when something in our own lives resonates to the same experience, when something within ourselves "recognizes" something similar in the life of Jesus.

In this sense, to contemplate major moments in our own lives is to contemplate the life of Jesus.

Conversely, to contemplate something of great moment in the life of Jesus is to find ourselves wrestling with issues quite personal to our own lives.

This is merely suggesting that *his* heart and *our* hearts are not different.

In your mind's eye, imagine Jesus catching his first sight of Jerusalem as he comes over the hill! This is the city he has been avoiding out of fear. Yet it represents all his hopes. Watch him carefully as he stands or sits there, looking at this city that has captured his Jewish life in some profound way. He is beyond words. There are deep feelings moving within him. Tears begin to form in his eyes. Watch him quietly as you start to sense within yourself what he might be experiencing and feeling. Take your time to become aware of how moved he is, and of what is going through his mind and heart in front of this city of his people.

For Discussion

- Jesus stood alone against the tide. His work lay in ruins. He was facing utter failure.

    Discuss together the truth of this.

- Jesus never saw the blossoming of the Church—he did not experience their Pentecost. He simply chose to believe that the future lay totally in the hands of the Spirit he loved—whatever that might ultimately mean.

    What difference does this make to your understanding of his greatness?

    In the light of his courage and inner freedom as he approached Jerusalem, how do you see your own life?

- Jerusalem represented so much of Jesus' longings for justice. What would be one such Jerusalem in your own life?

16
Set Your Heart upon the Deep

The centurion, who was standing in front of him, had seen *how he had died,* and he said, "In truth this man was *Son of God.*"

Mark 15:39 (emphasis added)

When the centurion saw *what had taken place,* he gave praise to God and said, "Truly, this was *an upright man.*"

Luke 23:47 (emphasis added)

FROM OUR EARLIEST YEARS we learned that "Jesus saved us by his death on the cross." In an even older theology, the words would go something like this: "By his death, Jesus opened for us the gates of heaven."

Now these are true statements, but the language is so theologically packed that many of us spend years of our lives not knowing *what they mean in reality.*

How does the death of Jesus "save" *us?* And what was it that was "opened" to *us,* which the Church came to call "the gates of heaven"?

When we were young people in primary school, much of what we learned was a simplified theology. The teachings of the great theologians of the Church were broken down into digestible pieces for children to learn. We might have learned the *words,* but I suspect that for most of us the *meanings* of the words escaped us. As we grew older, what we had learned in religion class seemed to have little connection with real life. Many leave the Church when this happens.

The task upon us today is not so much to change the Church's teachings but to express those teachings about God, Jesus, and ourselves in a *language* that *makes sense* for people of today, in a *language* that connects with the world in which we now live.

Mark, who wrote the first of the gospels, was in no doubt as to what it means to say that Jesus "saves" us. The clue lies in the words we have quoted at the beginning of this chapter. When we realize what Mark was telling us by these simple words, the mystery of Jesus and of what he means for us today can totally overwhelm us.

In the whole of Mark's Gospel, Jesus was called "divine" only twice. In the opening sentence, Mark called him "Son of God"; so there was no doubt in Mark's mind about the reality of his divinity. The only other person to call Jesus "Son of God" was the pagan Roman centurion on Calvary. For the rest of the gospel, Mark carefully called Jesus "Son of man," a phrase that has also been translated as "the Human One."

In some ways the title "the Human One" is the whole point of Mark's Gospel. In this "human person" was cradled the likeness and energy of God. In this ordinary human person, who was portrayed by Mark as having to walk in faith as we do, being afraid as we sometimes are, needing to pray as we must, and as capable of discovering God in his life as we are, in this human one, said Mark, lies the hope for us all. If the spirit of God could so mature a person as human as Jesus, then indeed there is hope for us all. If it could happen to *one* of us, then the implications for *all* of us are awesome. And in Jesus, this ordinary human person, more like us than we dare to imagine, *it* happened.

It was on Calvary, when Jesus was finally face to face with death (something we all shall experience), that we catch a powerful insight into what "it" was that happened.

It was *the way* he died. Or, as the Roman centurion would say, it was "how he had died," the *manner of his dying.*

This Roman centurion was a professional soldier. He was in charge of this execution, so he was probably experienced in the task. He had seen many die in his lifetime, but he had never seen anyone die as this man died. There was no doubt in his mind: what he witnessed that afternoon just had to be "divine," so far was it beyond anything he had ever previously experienced. What he saw and heard that afternoon blew him away into the realm of God. Stunned by the courage and love of this Jesus whom he watched dying, he knew intuitively that he was in the presence of the sacred. He was a pagan, but the quality of Jesus' last hours on the cross shattered his pagan world and brought him into the realm of mystery and wonder.

What had he seen happening?

- The centurion saw a man crucified who chose not to hate in return. Under severe torment and mockery, he held his peace and refused to be goaded into responding with the hatred and violence of his accusers. He would not surrender to them his capacity to stay gentle and to keep loving—this was one thing they could not take away from him. He would not surrender the core of his human dignity. They would not crucify the image of God in which he was made. Nor would he demean that beautiful likeness by cursing or by anger.
- The soldier saw a man dying in great pain, but more concerned for two others who were hanging beside him. Jesus supported them with his words. He encouraged them with his own belief.
- The Roman watched a man being nailed to a cross, quietly begging his God, on the soldiers' behalf, for forgiveness. Had he ever seen a person who lived so far beyond the boundaries of self-concern? Even under torture, this

Jesus was reaching down into the depths of his being for a compassion that was more concerned for the violence the soldiers were *inflicting on themselves* in crucifying him. *"Father, forgive them, they do not know what it is they are doing"* (author's paraphrase).

- The centurion was touched by the tenderness of the crucified one for his mother and friends, moved by Jesus' loving concern for his mother's future and security.

- He listened while this dying Jew, gasping for breath, prayed one of the long-loved psalms of his childhood. And not just for himself did Jesus pray, for he prayed the psalms the way every Jew prayed the psalms—on behalf of his nation and his people. For Jewish people who prayed the psalms, the personal pronouns *I* or *me* or *myself* stood for the whole nation before God. So it was that Jesus prayed over his people, on behalf of his people: *"'My God, my God, why have you forsaken me?'"* (Mark 15:34).

  It was a prayer of the dying Jesus, tempted, as he had never been tempted before, to stop believing in his Father's tenderness, constant presence, and love. In his own private holocaust on the cross, and in the hellish life that he saw his beloved people choosing for themselves, how could he continue to believe in a God who loved, who cared, who was as close as one's breath?

  Yet Jesus prayed for himself and for his people. Like all who pray the psalms even today, the prayer is for all of us, like creation groaning to its God. The soldier saw this wonder: in the midst of his own anguish, Jesus was thinking of his people and praying for them, passionately.

- The centurion heard one final utterance. He would never know what it cost Jesus to pray this final, closing prayer of his life. Surrounded by every indication of God's absence and nonexistence, Jesus had to make one final choice, one irrevocable commitment. Either God *is* or God *isn't*. Jesus had either been totally, terribly wrong in his life, or God was still somehow here, somehow still the loving and tender God he had known as a child.

And in his last conscious moment, this his greatest moment, Jesus *chose to believe:* "Father, into your arms I throw my spirit" (author's paraphrase).

He launched his heart this one final time upon the deep. It was finished. It had been done. Completed. He proved himself faithful to the very end.

In this incredible fidelity to the God he knew in his life, Jesus demonstrated to all of us what we each carry deep within, *the capacity to keep loving.* No matter what the provocation, no matter what the circumstance and peril, that same quality of graciousness lies within us all. By the way he died, Jesus showed us the splendor and courage we all possess. Perhaps we would prefer not to know about it. Perhaps we would rather believe that it belonged only to himself in some special, divine way. We do not want to be so implicated, so challenged. But if he was "like us in all things," then truly we are involved. If one human person is capable of such love, then where does that leave the rest of us?

The death of Jesus "saves" us from missing the point of our lives. We cannot look properly at how he died without thereby seeing the depth of love and compassion of which we are all capable. It is ourselves we see; it is our potential that he embodies. The "depths of our inner heaven" are accessible to us when we look at the way he died—those gates are open! In seeing him, we see more than simply Jesus. His death confronts us with a crisis of belief in our own capacities and lives. The divine depths we see in him abide likewise in all of us no matter our culture, our religion, our personal history, our failures or circumstances. In him the graciousness of the human person has dawned for all to see. We are bearers, all of us, of the divine.

This is no more than Jesus believed: constructed in the very likeness of God, we will never be free until that likeness is released in our lives. This is salvation and redemption and *good* news. It is a message of hope that *all* have a right to hear.

For Prayer

Watching Jesus as he dies is possibly one of the most sacred of the Church's prayer traditions.

Different gospels record different moments as he hung on the cross for those three afternoon hours.

In your imagination, be there yourself like the centurion. It's like allowing yourself to daydream the things you then see and hear, the things you notice and remember.

In a quiet, unhurried way, allow yourself to watch, to notice, and to "hear" *one* of the profound moments mentioned above.

For Discussion

- "By his death we are saved and set free." What does this mean for us today? How can *his* death be said to free *us?*
- "He is the image of the unseen God,
  the first-born of all creation..." (Colossians 1:15).
  What do these words of Saint Paul now mean for you?
- Saint Paul said that when we were baptized, we were baptized *into his death*. Using the above story for data, discuss what Paul might have meant. How does this change the way you see baptism in your life?

17
Line of Fire

"...I am telling you the truth:
it is for your own good that I am going,
because *unless I go,*
the Paraclete will not come to you...."

John 16:7 (emphasis added)

...and there appeared to them tongues as of fire; these separated and
came to rest on the head of each of them. They were all filled with
the Holy Spirit and began to speak different languages *as the Spirit
gave them power* to express themselves.

Acts 2:3–4 (emphasis added)

WHILE THE CHURCH'S TRADITION often focuses on the resurrection of
Jesus, let us not lose sight of the resurrection of *his disciples.* What
occurred in their transformation is incredible.

Jesus was dead. The disciples were crushed by this realization.
This last, turbulent week had ended in the horror of his death.
Their own people had murdered him. The disciples were afraid,
discredited, and beaten.

They had lost heart, for Jesus had seemed to be the one hope for
the nation. His life and teaching seemed to fulfill their every Jewish
dream about themselves, about God, and about life. He was the
embodiment of justice and human dignity; he had spoken a truth
that they had recognized in the depths of their hearts. When Jesus had
spoken of God, a fire had burned inside them. He had been like a

rising sun in the morning of their lives—and now he was gone. The world was empty. They were shocked, broken, and deeply disillusioned.

Then something happened: Jesus rose, and something likewise rose within themselves. The disciples became aware that Jesus was living. They experienced his presence, and they named it resurrection.

The effect in their lives was simply incredible. One moment they were cowed and beaten, dispirited and broken. The next they were transformed into energetic, fearless, and dangerous disciples. *How* this occurred is not our concern—but *that* it occurred stirs something deep within our own hearts and minds. Once filled with the same sort of spirit that drove Jesus, the disciples burst onto the world, scattering fire in all directions and changing lives with an effect that Jesus in his life never seemed to achieve. This explosion of energy and confidence was a transformation in ordinary men and women that was in some ways far more startling and dangerous than what we have known as "the resurrection of Jesus." What happened to Jesus in his resurrection is a mystery beyond us. But what happened to these ordinary men and women is something we can understand and indeed experience in our own lives.

Let's consider what occurred.

- The disciples emerged from hiding and took to the streets fearlessly. We suddenly find old wishy-washy Peter taking it right up to the Jewish crowd, eye to eye and nose to nose: "'...make no mistake about this, but listen carefully to what I say....the Lord and Christ whom God has made is this Jesus whom you crucified'" (Acts 2:14, 36).
- Peter and John went into the very Temple to pray: the Temple—the scene of some of the fiercest confrontations between Jesus and the authorities. There they met a lame man on the steps. It was the man with the withered hand all over again! But note the new-found confidence of *this*

Peter, the hide of the man as he faced the cripple who had asked for money: "'I have neither silver nor gold, but I will give you what I have: in the name of Jesus Christ the Nazarene, walk!'" (Acts 3:6).

- His action caused great excitement; a crowd gathered, and as he did on Pentecost morning, Peter faced them with fire in his eye: "'...why are you so surprised at this? Why are you staring at *us*...? [This is all about] Jesus whom you handed over and then disowned in the presence of Pilate....It was you who accused the Holy and Upright One...you killed the prince of life!'" (Acts 3:12–16; emphasis added).

- Peter's words provoked an uproar in the Temple courtyard. The Sadducees and the Temple guard became involved. Arrested, Peter and John were brought before the very Sanhedrin that had plotted the death of their Jesus. Were they afraid of the Sanhedrin? Not on your life! Peter gave *them* a piece of his mind and presumed to lecture them about Jesus as well. The Sanhedrin were astonished at what was happening in front of their eyes— they had never seen the likes of this in their lives! "They were astonished at the fearlessness shown by Peter and John, considering that they were uneducated laymen; and they recognised them as associates of Jesus..." (Acts 4:13).

So they decided to frighten Peter and John with a fair warning: on no account were they to teach in the name of Jesus. Now this was all Peter needed—if they wanted a fight, he'd give them one! He stood up to them, as cool as you like: "'You must judge whether in God's eyes it is right to listen to you and not to God. We cannot stop proclaiming what we have seen and heard'" (Acts 4:19).

Far from frightened, the apostles took to the streets again, in utter defiance of the Sanhedrin's warning. Again they were arrested and jailed, yet managed to escape from prison during the night. The Sanhedrin, meeting next morning to decide their fate, found to their consternation that the apostles were not in jail where they should have been, but at that very moment "'in the Temple. They are standing there preaching to the people'" (Acts 5:25)! It was too much for the Sanhedrin—they again had them arrested and brought before the Council: "'We gave you a strong warning...not to preach in this name, and what have you done? You have filled Jerusalem with your teaching...'" (Acts 5:28).

Peter, the old fisherman, far from being awed by their power and prestige, was equal to the moment: "'Obedience to God comes before obedience to men...'" (Acts 5:29).

Was this the same Peter we met in the gospel stories? Something incredible had happened to this man. His language and courage went far beyond the language and fight even in Jesus. As a result of this head-on collision with the Sanhedrin, they were flogged and warned again, but they left "glad to have had the honour of suffering humiliation for the sake of the name" (Acts 5:41).

- Almost overnight, the disciples began to embody as a community an attitude of mind that had seemed way beyond them while Jesus was alive. These were the disciples who had argued as to which of them was the greatest, vying for places of honor in the kingdom of Jesus, and what do we now see? "And all who shared the faith owned everything in common; they sold their goods and possessions and distributed the proceeds among themselves according to what each one needed....they shared their food gladly and generously..." (Acts 2:44–46).
- Within a few months, the first of these believers laid down

his life for the same truth for which Jesus had died. Stephen, someone young and on fire with the liberating truth of the message of Jesus, was seen dying under a hail of stones and praying exactly the same prayer with which Jesus, his Lord, had died. He died as Jesus had died with the same love, the same concern for his accusers, the same plea for his beloved people: "'Lord, do not hold this sin against them'" (Acts 7:60).

- The Church began to face issues and questions that were far beyond anything Jesus had had to face in his life, including the thorny issue of what shape the young Church should take as it spread into cultures and nations that were no longer Jewish. This crucial meeting in Jerusalem is described in the fifteenth chapter of Acts. But according to Paul, the issue was a fiery one—the Church's first—and one that almost split them right down the center. The argument was head to head: "...when Cephas came to Antioch, then I did oppose him to his face since he was manifestly in the wrong....I said to Cephas in front of all of them, 'Since you, though you are a Jew, live like the gentiles and not like the Jews, how can you compel the gentiles to live like the Jews?'" (Galatians 2:11–14).

Jesus had come "to cast fire on the earth," and look at what was happening: the disciples had "caught" something from him, some spark that ignited a spirit deep within themselves. No wonder Jesus would see himself as needing almost to get out of the way of their lives:

> ...it is for your own good that I am going,
> because unless I go,
> the Paraclete will not come to you....
> John 16:7

It was as if Jesus knew in his heart that for as long as they saw *him* as the one who possessed the Spirit, then to that degree they were blind to the Spirit lurking within their own beings. Fascinated by him, they were unable to look for Spirit within themselves.

It was the belief of Jesus that all possess such Spirit. The basis of his lovely Jewish faith was that all are made in the image and likeness of God. We can speak of the Spirit of God as something we need to "receive," and we can equally speak about that Spirit as something we are desperate to "uncover" within ourselves. It is uncovered only by love. It will emerge from our deepest hearts only when the space is created for it to do so. The space for Spirit is given to us whenever we are surrounded by the love of those who believe it lies within us.

Then, as happened to the disciples at Pentecost, Spirit will burn in us like true baptism. We will then take our rightful and dignified places alongside those apostles and alongside Jesus in the line of fire sweeping the earth. Then, and only then, will we again begin to speak the "languages of the world" in ways intelligible to all human hearts: *To be on earth the heart of God.*

For Prayer

There is a lovely tradition in Church prayer of reading the Scriptures. Not in any hurried way, but at a leisurely, reflective pace. There is a special Latin name for such prayerful pondering: it is called *lectio divina* (sacred reading).

The art is to be *attentive*. We set ourselves to notice movements of our own spirit within as we let the words and stories of the Scriptures trickle past our mind's eye. Does some sentence stir an excitement in me? Do some words begin to disturb me? Do I find some aspect of the text attractive for some reason? In other words, my inner eye is fixed on my reactions and responses to what I am reading with my "outer" eyes.

When I notice some movement within myself, I stop and pay attention to that. I dwell on it, taste it.

Might I suggest such a prayerful and slow reading of two chapters of the Acts of the Apostles. Chapters three and four are filled with images of a Peter who is on fire. Let the experience of this simple man speak to you.

For Discussion

- The Spirit of God that burst out of Peter and the disciples is something all human beings possess. It lies hidden within, and most suspect nothing of its presence. Our role as parents, educators, or ministers is not so much to bring the Spirit to people, but to help them uncover the Spirit already *within* themselves.

  Discuss the implications of such an outlook for our lives as Church. What does this say to us about our mission in the world of today?

- "'Unless I go, the Spirit cannot come'" (John 16:7, author's paraphrase).

  Discuss what this meant in the life of Jesus and what it might mean in our own lives.

Conclusion

> The split between the faith which many people profess and their daily lives deserves to be counted among the more serious errors of our age.

THIS INSIGHT FROM VATICAN II's document *The Church in the Modern World* (43) is both the starting and finishing point of this book. In these transitional, uncertain times, the one thing we must recover with confidence is the story that alone provides meaning, context, and energy for living. Our belief has always been that in the life of this person, Jesus of Nazareth, the full bridging of the gap between life and faith was realized. He alone "passed over" completely into God. In him the destiny of all was embodied. In him the "hidden self" of which Paul spoke (and which we all possess) grew strong; it emerged to be seen by all.

Yet strangely, how rarely do we speak with one another about the person he was.

The task upon us is to find a more down-to-earth language through which to describe this down-to-earth God; to glimpse the person underlying the Church's theology, so as to grasp the theology underlying our own personhood.

Without this sense of the sacredness of humanity—his and ours—we will never sense the awesome dignity that surrounds all of life and all of creation. Either God is here or not here. Everything hangs on the emphasis we choose.

God, we praise you;
You reveal yourself in the depths of our being,
drawing us to share in your life and your love.
Be near to the people formed in your image,
close to the world your love brings to life.

                    Opening Prayer for Trinity Sunday

About the Author

A MISSIONARY OF THE SACRED HEART, Father Andersen has studied at the Institute for Spirituality and Worship at the Jesuit School of Theology, Berkeley, California, and at the Pontifical Liturgical Institute of San Anselmo, Rome. He is widely known for his retreat and adult faith-education work. He has been involved in parish formation and renewal programs, staff faith development, liturgical workshops, ministerial formation courses, and clergy renewal in-services. He is one of the most popular composers of modern hymns in Australia and currently works in adult formation programs out of Melbourne, Australia.

More great titles from Triumph™ Books...

IMPRESSIONS OF A LIFE
Stories of Jesus
Denis McBride, Foreword by Joseph F. Girzone

"This is a book everyone would enjoy reading. A work of art."
—Joseph F. Girzone, author of *Joshua*

A neighbor...a child...a friend...an adulteress...a secret agent. These are among the 15 Gospel men and women from all walks of life whose stories and impressions of the Jesus they knew—whether up close or from afar—are told here with riveting honesty and an immediacy that speaks to contemporary readers. **$15.95**

SACRED READING
The Ancient Art of *Lectio Divina*
Michael Casey

"Reflective personal reading is rapidly becoming a lost art. Michael Casey invites contemporary Christians to practice the ancient discipline of lectio divina as a way of deepening communion with God and with others. Spending time with *Sacred Reading* is itself an exercise in holy reading."
—Michael Downey, Editor, *The New Dictionary of Catholic Spirituality*

$12.95

REDISCOVERING MARY
Insights from the Gospels
Tina Beattie

Rediscovering Mary is a compelling series of reflections that show how a new appreciation of Mary, as presented in the Bible, can inspire us to rethink such issues as power, wealth, love, loyalty, and family. Fresh insights of Mary's actual roles in biblical events, such as the Annunciation, the Visitation, the birth of Jesus, the wedding at Cana, and the Crucifixion, appear on every page. **$9.95**

THE JESUS WE KNEW
James R. Jennings

Here are three distinctive and dramatic accounts of what it was like to follow Jesus in the Palestine of his day. A compelling book and a vivid recreation of Gospel events that changed the course of history! **$15.95**

Order from your local bookstore or write to:
Liguori Publications
Box 060, Liguori, MO 63057-9999

(Please add $2 for postage and handling for prepaid orders $9.99 and under; $3 for orders between $10 and $14.99; $4 for orders $15 and over.)